TALK TO ME I'M GRIEVING

"This is a must-read for anyone grieving a loss. Barbara offers a compelling look into grief based on her own personal experiences. It serves as the most complete, thoughtful, and useful "handbook" I have encountered, offering insight and tools for grieving and those wanting to help."

—MaryEllen Lowrey, executive director TIP Orange County

"This should be required reading for all humans. It gives readers validation and permission to feel. Grieving people will find respite, empathy, and insight into their own emotions and experience. People who are supporting the grieving will get answers to the questions they've always had but have been afraid to ask."

—Dr. Madeline Smith, bestselling author of *Whole Lotta $$$ in this MoFo: An Employer's Guide to Navigating Legalized Larceny Within American Healthcare*

"Barbara's first book, *Keven's Choice*, blew my mind and taught me of an unconditional love I did not know existed. This book shows me how not to be afraid of my own or anyone's grief and how to name it and walk with others. I am so grateful to learn from her and call her a friend."

—Korey Pollard, storyteller, actor, producer, author

"Barbara Legere's book, *Talk To Me I am Grieving,* is an incredible resource for those of us grieving and those who know people grieving the loss of a loved one. Legere shares invaluable advice that we can all use at different times in our personal journeys. This is a must-read for everyone, regardless of age. Thank you, Barbara, for touching my heart like you have and helping me on my grieving journey."

—Chuck Thuss, podcast host of *Warriors Unmasked*

"Talk to Me I'm Grieving transcends boundaries, resonating with individuals from all walks of life, inviting them to embrace their pain, honor their emotions, and embark on a transformative journey toward healing and growth. Through practical tools, personal anecdotes, and timeless wisdom, this book helps readers navigate tumultuous emotions while supporting those experiencing grief in its many forms. Author Barbara Legere is the epitome of turning one's pain into purpose."

—Jessie Buttafuoco, MA, trauma-informed media consultant

"Barbara Legere's *Talk to Me I'm Grieving* is straight from the heart. It is raw, it is real, and it is incredibly insightful. This book shows us the nitty gritty truth from all perspectives and angles so we can best support those we love. It is my hope that these pages get into as many hands as possible."

—Sara ONeil, author of *When the F Will He Text*

"Through her own unimaginable grief, Barbara Legere provides a rare and essential guide where it is most needed. In a culture that often avoids and looks for ways to get over grief,

Legere invites the reader to not only have a conversation about it but also make space for and have a relationship with it. Whether your grief or in support of others, Legere has written a companion to return to in times of loss and great sorrow. *Talk to Me I'm Grieving* is a gift."

—Hannah Sward, critically acclaimed author of *Strip: A Memoir*

"Barbara writes about grief with the spirit of a calm, wise, caring guide. When reading her words, you know she's been there; you know she's struggled; you know she will have something to say to you in your grief. Then she makes it even better: she includes the words of others from all angles of grief—even the death of a pet. It's as thorough and practical a treatment of grief as you will find."

—Ken Guidroz, author of *Letters to My Son in Prison*

"Barbara Legere provides useful tools for what to do and say when anyone has lost a loved one. Legere has first-hand experience with how people act in these cases, often incorrectly. *Talk to Me I'm Grieving* sets the bar in handling a difficult situation."

—Timothy Gager, author of 18 books and the bestseller *Joe the Salamander*

"*Talk to Me I'm Grieving* presents an unforgettable journey through the intricate labyrinth of loss. Profoundly insightful, Legere balances candid honesty with tender empathy, boldly challenging clichés to offer a fresh, empowering perspective on grief that encourages authenticity and healing. The book stands as a powerful testament to the enduring capacity of love beyond life's finale, seamlessly weaving a compelling narrative that makes it an essential addition to every bookshelf."

—Jordan P. Barnes, author of *One Hit Away: A Memoir of Recovery*

"Stunningly raw and piercingly authentic. Legere curates a robust mosaic of her own profoundly heart-shattering tragedy and the grief stories experienced by her fellow wounded healers. Legere's book resonates with anyone in any phase of the grieving process and guides those who never know what to say or how to support someone in crisis. Readers will find practical advice, solace, empathy, and guidance through all areas of accepting life after loss."

—Amy Liz Harrison, bestselling author of *Eternally Expecting: A Mom Gets Sober and Gives Birth to a Whole New Life...Her Own*

"The book this culture needs! We all know grief in one way or another, but what to do with it is something that many of us have never figured out. The pages in this book are the truth, honesty, and vulnerability of how to cope with grief and show up for those grieving."

—Samantha Perkins, author of the bestselling memoir *Alive AF-One Anxious Mom's Journey To Becoming Alcohol Free.*

"*Talk to Me I'm Grieving* offers insight into grief and how a family member or friend can better understand the process when someone they know is grieving. You will benefit by reading *Talk to Me I'm Grieving,* because not only will you better understand the griever, but you will also discover the verbal tools as to what to say when someone loses a loved one, as well as find several resources."

—Jodi Barber, producer of *Overtaken* documentary

"All seven billion of us will grieve. How can we talk about this with one another? In *Talk to Me I'm Grieving*, Legere educates us and destigmatizes this deeply human emotion and does so with compassion born of her own losses. The author brings to the surface a human condition we all experience and often suffer with alone. She speaks directly and eloquently to two groups— those grieving and those who care about them and just don't know what to say. She makes it imminently clear that grief is love."

—Shuna Morelli, founder of the BodyMind Bridge Institute and bestselling author of the *BodyMind Bridge* series

"Barbara masterfully shatters limiting paradigms about how a grieving person should be treated in this short yet comprehensive book. She provides practical tools to navigate the wide variety of pain that can be experienced through loss and the way people respond to it. *Talk To Me I'm Grieving* is a vital body of work that is nothing less than a divine light."

—Kevin Carton, international teacher, speaker, & transformational life coach

Talk to Me I'm Grieving

Talk to Me I'm Grieving

Supportive Ways to Help Someone Through Grief

Barbara Legere

EMPOWERED PRESS

Talk To Me I'm Grieving is a work of non fiction. Names and identifying details of certain individuals mentioned in this book have been changed in order to protect their privacy.

Library of Congress Control Number: 2023938651

ISBN: 978-1-957430-16-4 (paperback)

ISBN: 978-1-957430-18-8 (ebook)

Published by the Empowered Press in Las Cruces, NM

http://www.theempoweredpress.com

publish@theempoweredpress.com

Cover design: Onur Aksoy

Onegraphica.com

Layout: Jill Carlyle

Dedicated to my aunt, Sister Margaret Lucille, whose unconditional love and compassion have been a model for me throughout my life.

Each person's grief is as unique as their fingerprint. But what everyone has in common is no matter how they grieve, they share a need for their grief to be witnessed. It doesn't mean needing someone to lessen it or reframe it for them. The need is for someone to be fully present to the magnitude of their loss without trying to point out the silver lining.

— DAVID KESSLER

CONTENTS

FOREWORD

I met Barbara Legere in the spring of 2021 when we were both members of a very special online writing community. The world was in the throes of the Covid pandemic amidst a lockdown, and Barbara had lost her only child six months earlier. At the time, we lived on separate coasts of the US–Barbara in Southern California and me in Central Florida. We would have never met if it hadn't been for our passion for telling stories that matter. And I would have missed out on knowing a precious human and cultivating a lifelong friendship.

At the time, Barbara had just begun working on her first book. She didn't yet have a title for it; she just knew that through her tragic loss, she would use her experiences to advocate for others suffering from substance use disorders, mental health, and grief. I was privileged to watch Barbara's story evolve into the bestselling memoir *Keven's Choice: A Mother's Journey Through Her Son's Mental Illness and Suicide*; more importantly, I have watched Barbara transform her heartache into healing and unconditional support for other grieving people.

I remember Barbara telling me she would "never write another book," but I knew she had more to share with the world. So, I wasn't surprised when I found out she'd written the book you're holding in your hands right now. At the heart of this book is the recognition that grief cannot simply be "fixed." It is a process, a journey, and a form of love that never truly goes away. Barbara offers a roadmap that acknowledges the reality of grief while also providing concrete steps for navigating its challenges.

For those who are grieving, this book offers practical advice on self-care, coping strategies, and honoring the memory of their loved ones. For those supporting someone grieving, it provides insight into how to be there for them. *Talk to Me I'm Grieving* acknowledges the pain and sadness of loss while also offering a path forward.

Barbara has a way with words. She has a special gift of making every reader feel like they are sitting together, sharing coffee over conversations. So if you're looking for a book that makes you feel seen and heard and assures you that you are not alone, you will not be disappointed.

I am honored to introduce this book not only as its publisher but Barbara's good friend. I hope it will be a source of comfort and guidance for all who read it.

Jill Carlyle, MA, MFA
Publisher, Empowered Press

INTRODUCTION

Our culture is not comfortable with death or grief. When we don't know what to say, we rely on platitudes or avoid being around the grieving person. It's not our fault, and very few people talk about it. As a mother who has lost her son, please know most of us grievers want to talk about our losses, especially when we lose a child. Hearing their name is music to our ears.

While writing these guidelines, I heard voices: fathers, mothers, sisters, brothers, grandparents, and friends. Voices of the loved ones left behind after a stillbirth, suicide, illness, old age, accident, overdose, or fentanyl death.

The voices called out, "I am hurting. I feel alone. Please talk to me about my loss. I need to share what I'm going through. Please don't abandon me!"

Over the years, I've had the privilege of communicating with hundreds of grievers about their losses. When no one talks about their loss, grievers feel forgotten. Friends and family fear bringing up the loss will remind them of their loved one and make them sad all over again—grievers long for acknowledgment. When loss goes unrecognized or is treated as a cliché, it adds a layer of pain. Validating the loss with words or actions says to the griever, "I see you, and I understand why you're hurting. I am on your side."

Grief is unique—it differs from person to person. There isn't a specific way to grieve or a standard amount of time to process the loss. Those closest to us hate to see us suffer, want our grief to end, and do what they think is best to help us "get over it." But the truth is, losing a loved one isn't something you ever get over.

What is grief? Grief is love. The more we love the person, the harder we grieve when we lose them. Grief never leaves us, but it will progress to where we can live within it. Eventually, it *is* possible for us to laugh, love, and be happy again. I like to think of grief in two stages, "early" and "forever." We need support from friends and family to get through both stages—more on that in later chapters.

I wrote this book with you in mind. My friends helped me understand the types of grief I wasn't familiar with. To speak of grief as a whole, I included stories from personal friends who understand the pain of losing a sibling, friend, spouse, job, pet, etc. You will hear from them throughout the book; their stories are a *vital* part of this book, and I am grateful for them.

STORIES OF LOSS:

- Loss of a Child—Laura Swank
- Loss of a Sibling—Ellie Markes
- Loss of a Parent—Paul Lesinski
- Loss of a Spouse/Life Partner—Margie Allman
- Loss of a Friend—Mike Duffy

- Loss to Suicide—Harv Jamison
- Loss to Murder—Stephanie Swanson
- Loss of the Living—Bob Edwards
- Loss to a Life-Changing Illness—Lee Varon
- Loss of a Future—Donna Van Horn
- Loss of a Pet—Heidi Le

Throughout their lives, these friends have experienced a variety of grief. They've opened their hearts here to share how grief affects us differently. Ellie shares about losing her brother, who was also her best friend. Margie shares how the unexpected death of her life partner left her with grief and guilt. Stephanie talks about what it's like to lose a son who was unarmed, shot, and killed by the police. Heidi talks about losing a beloved pet, something many of us can relate to.

There is a different side to grief in each of their stories. Without their input, this book would not be as valuable. It takes courage and vulnerability to share from the heart; I'm so grateful to each of them.

One thing I hope you take away from this book is that grief is not only about the person who died but also about the person who loved them, lost them, and must go on without them. You play a crucial role in their healing journey.

HOW TO READ THIS BOOK

It's unnecessary to read every chapter of this book in order. They include stories to help readers understand what grief feels like for different people in different situations. For those that are only interested in what to say/do to help a grieving person, Part Four provides that information.

Note: Because of the opiate epidemic, the fentanyl crisis, and rising suicide rates, I've included special chapters on these sensitive types of losses. They're more difficult to talk about but just as important to acknowledge. Grievers of these types of deaths are often overlooked or considered "unworthy" of the same amount of compassion.

PART ONE

MY PERSONAL EXPERIENCE WITH GRIEF

CHAPTER 1
WHY SHOULD YOU LISTEN TO ME?

Time is precious. This becomes even more obvious after you lose someone you deeply love. The most significant and profound loss of my life was my son, Keven. Keven died by suicide on August 11, 2020. Five years before Kev's death, I lost Anthony, Keven's best friend, whom I refer to as my "heart son." I call him this because I loved him with all my heart, even though I didn't give birth to him. I've written two bonus chapters located at the end of this book that I hope you'll take the time to read. You'll get to know these two amazing young men and their stories.

Whenever I read nonfiction, I make sure what I'm learning is worth my time. I respect your time, so this book is short and to the point. After reading it, you will know what grieving people long to hear, why, and what they hope they never hear again.

After losing my son, I noticed people offering me their clichéd condolences, which were often more hurtful than helpful; I paid attention and asked others about their experiences with grief. As a result, I've talked to or read comments from hundreds of people, and most feel "grief" clichés are unthoughtful and hollow. To gain a diverse perspective, I observed a variety of people. Most of us experience grief and long for comfort in similar ways, but we don't all express it the same way.

In observing teens and young adults, I noticed distractions helped them avoid feeling their loss. I remember doing the same thing when I lost my father as a teen. It was easier to numb my pain with drugs, alcohol, and constantly being with friends than to face it. I wasn't ready to allow myself to feel such deep feelings.

I noticed that in the generation before mine (I'm at the tail end of baby boomers), some men still feel uncomfortable crying and choose to shut down rather than express their emotions. I've seen guys express their sadness as anger (swearing, punching a wall) while others share their feelings openly.

Even though women are more likely to cry and share their feelings, men are more open these days. Thankfully, the "men don't cry" ideology is declining.

Some people like to publicly share their grief (for example, wearing a t-shirt with their loved one's name), and others avoid talking about it. It's not uncommon to get a remembrance tattoo, especially in child loss. We're all unique. There are no rules for grieving.

Additionally, I learned there are sixteen types of grief. When I read the descriptions, some overlapped and added complications rather than clarification. They are:

1. Normal Grief
2. Anticipatory Grief
3. Complicated Grief
4. Chronic Grief
5. Delayed Grief

6. Distorted Grief
7. Cumulative Grief
8. Exaggerated Grief
9. Secondary Loss
10. Masked Grief
11. Disenfranchised Grief (Ambiguous)
12. Traumatic Grief
13. Collective Grief
14. Inhibited Grief
15. Abbreviated Grief
16. Absent Grief

While we all grieve differently, many of our feelings are the same:

- Devastated
- Heartbroken
- Lost
- Forever Changed
- Empty
- Sick
- Numb

It's important to know that we are not at fault for using the clichés we've heard all our lives. I've been using them too, and it wasn't until losing Keven and Anthony that I experienced firsthand what it felt like to be on the receiving end of traditional condolence phrases. My hope for this book is to provide some alternative ways to support someone who's grieving.

CHAPTER 2

GRIEF FOUND ME AT AN EARLY AGE

I experienced grief for the first time when I lost my Aunt Ellen. I was five years old. Aunt Ellen died of an unknown illness; she was only forty-five. In the 60s, we didn't have the diagnostic technology we have today, so her death remains a mystery. As a child, I spent a lot of time with Aunt Ellen; we were very close, and it was hard to accept she was gone forever. When it finally registered that I would never see her again, I lost some of the carefree innocence most kids have. After her death, I always expected another tragic event to be right around the corner, and in the grand scheme of things, it was.

Nearly a decade later, my father was diagnosed with lung cancer. It was the 70s, and cancer treatment hadn't advanced very far. I will never forget walking into my parents' bedroom near the end of my father's life. His shirt was off, and the "exploratory surgery" scars on his body caused trauma to my loving eyes. It looked like they had cut his whole body open. It seemed barbaric to me. After three years of treatment, my beloved father passed away. I was a daddy's girl through and through, and it still hurts to think back on the pain and suffering he endured all those years ago.

In my family, we rarely expressed emotions or talked about feelings, so I had to figure these things out on my own. I'd already started partying with my friends at age thirteen, but now my weekend "fun" turned into daily drug use (mainly smoking weed) and drinking, and then I'd blackout. I had a distorted view of sex, and as a result, I was extremely promiscuous, which led to feelings of shame and disappointment in myself that I carried with me far into adulthood. Years of negative self-talk directly resulted from my behavior and affected my relationships with men.

Two years after losing my dad, I experienced another devastating loss. My close friend, Steve, died by suicide when I was seventeen. His friends and family knew he was suicidal. He told his brother, John, me, and a few other people. We tried our best to ensure he was always with someone.

I spent the entire day with him before he passed, and his brother stayed by his side that night. The following day, we were all going to a Christmas party at a friend's house in San Diego, an hour from where we lived. Steve told me he was going to the party with his brother and told his brother he was coming with me. When we realized he'd tricked us, his brother immediately drove back to check on him, but it was too late. When I heard the news, I was hysterical and blamed myself. Years later, I learned Steve displayed all the classic signs of schizophrenia. I finally let go of my guilt for being unable to "save" him.

In the years following Steve's death, I lost two family members to suicide. My cousin Armond had come home from the Vietnam War addicted to heroin and traumatized by the violence he witnessed. He took his life a few years after returning. For those too young to remember, they often scorned

Vietnam veterans when they returned from the unpopular war. We didn't show them the honor and respect we offer to current Veterans.

My cousins were much older than me, so I didn't know them well; however, I felt very close to my cousin Tom. He was going through a divorce and felt like he had lost everything. His father found him in the garage after he attempted suicide by carbon dioxide. Tom was still alive but sustained severe brain damage and was institutionalized for the rest of his life. Losing him hit me hard. It devastated all of us who loved him. My aunt never genuinely smiled again.

In my 40s, I lost one of my best friends, Doug, to suicide. He lived in Canada, and we chatted almost every night via phone or Yahoo Messenger. We'd met in an online forum for people who suffered from depression, so it wasn't an unusual topic for us.

"Barbie," he said (he was the only person allowed to call me this. I called him 'Dougie'), "my life is the opposite of what I wanted for myself. I don't even like my job anymore. Sometimes I wonder if it's even worth it. I love my kids but let them down by cheating on their mom. They will never look at me the same again."

"Dougie, everyone makes mistakes, and you've asked for forgiveness. There's nothing else you can do. Your kids will probably come around in time. You're an amazing human being, and you're one of my best friends; I *need* you. What can I do to help? Do you want me to fly up there for a visit?" I asked.

He declined my offer. I continued to encourage Doug by reminding him that people in his life loved him, including his two children and me. It crossed my mind that he considered ending his life, but I didn't know how serious he was or what else I could do besides suggesting therapy and medication.

I noticed he slowly gave away or sold many of his possessions, even his cherished 1978 red Corvette. He sold his house, moved into a condo, and made memory scrapbooks for his teenage children. Those were all obvious signs of contemplating suicide, but I was still shocked to get the news.

After his death, his sister called me. She and Doug weren't close, so she didn't know who I was.

"Doug left a note for both his children and one for you." She read it to me, and I sat and wept, feeling like I had let him down. I couldn't believe he was gone. I felt lonely and sad every evening around the time we usually talked. He was suffering much more than I had realized, and I had to fight the type of guilt I felt after losing Steve almost twenty years before. Doug was like a big brother to me, and I still miss him.

In 2002 I lost my close friend Denice to breast cancer. She was forty-two years old. Denice and I met on the job and spent our lunch hours together most days. We were both pregnant with our first (and only) child at the same time. Our boys became friends. When I think of her, the first thing that comes to mind is her sensitivity, kindness, and generosity. But unless you knew her well, these traits remained hidden under her dry sense of humor. Denice was *so* funny! With her sharp wit and sense of fun, she holds the record for making me laugh the hardest I've ever laughed in my entire life.

Several weeks before she died, I visited Denice in the hospital and accidentally walked past her room. I peeked inside as I walked by, but she'd become unrecognizable in her last weeks of suffering. I thought they had moved an elderly woman into her room, so I kept walking until the shocking truth hit me—that was Denice. As we sat and talked that last time, it was December 1999. With her typical humor, she said, "Don't worry, I'm not kicking the bucket yet; I'm gonna stick around to see if this Y2K BS is real!" She had me laughing even as she lay dying. She lived until January 2000.

Throughout the years, I eventually lost all four grandparents, my mom, thirteen aunts, fifteen uncles, and three more cousins, plus other friends, to a heart attack, drug overdose, and cancer.

Then, the two most devastating losses of my life: Anthony and, five years later, my son, Keven.

PART TWO

ABOUT GRIEF

CHAPTER 3
GRIEF

Let me start by thanking you for setting aside time to learn how to support and understand someone in grief. Grieving friends and family may not think to thank you, but they'll be grateful that you provided comfort and support and allowed them to express their grief openly.

There's no end to grief. Grief isn't something we get over; we walk through it (or crawl or stumble). But, we eventually adjust to our new "normal" without the person we lost. Grief isn't over, but it's different.

I hesitate to say "it gets easier" because there is nothing easy about it, but it does, for most people, become more manageable. For example, I no longer cry every time I go grocery shopping and see items I would buy Keven, but I still feel sad. My heart-wrenching pain is less frequent, but it still occurs. Now I can laugh easier, sleep better, and even make it several days without feeling empty. But I still miss him every second of every day. In the beginning, I thought I could never again enjoy a concert, get excited about an event, or experience genuine joy. But now, I can.

The way a death "happens" also influences grief. Part Three will discuss different losses, for example, the death of a spouse, a sibling, or a friend. Regardless of the cause, it'll fall into one of these two categories: sudden or expected.

SUDDEN DEATH

The death that catches you off guard. A sudden, unanticipated death will leave you traumatized on top of your grief. You may also be in shock besides being debilitated by grief. This doesn't mean it will hurt more. An expected death hurts just as much but without the element of surprise. The term "it brought me to my knees" describes it well. When Keven died, I literally dropped to my knees and screamed his name.

If you experience a traumatic death, an accident, an overdose, suicide, or murder, there are resources at the back of the book for further reading. Trauma has a unique recovery all its own.

EXPECTED DEATH

Losing someone to a life-threatening or terminal illness is painful. Seeing your loved one's health decline is devastating. When someone's dying, whether or not they're conscious, myriad emotions rise to the surface: sadness, anxiety, sorrow, depression, anger, helplessness, fear, guilt, stress, and worry.

At some point, you may think, "I hope they go soon to end their suffering." This is common. Your thought was generous; you were thinking of them, not yourself. Try not to feel guilty.

One day, I was looking out the kitchen window at Keven. A cigarette and a lighter were in one hand as he was passed out in a chair in the backyard. Because he felt hopeless, he numbed himself with drugs to keep going. As I watched him, the thought came to my mind, “Maybe he’s right; maybe he would be better off dead.” For weeks, I felt horrified. How could I think such a thing? That thought haunted me regularly after he was gone, but I learned to see it for what it was—a thought. Not a wish, not something I wanted, just a thought.

People in deep grief notice when those around them are uncomfortable. They rarely discuss the loss after the initial condolences. No one enjoys seeing us sad, depressed, or crying; they want us to be like we used to be. So when we're suffering, some of us put on our "happy face” to make others feel better.

Some people said things after Keven died that hurt or put me on the defense. For example, several months after he passed, someone told me to “snap out of it” because I shared pictures of him on Facebook. It was an outrageous thing to say, but I didn’t get mad. I believe the person was really saying, “I can’t stand seeing you suffer so openly and expressing your pain in public. Looking at all your Facebook posts with pictures of your son is painful. I’m sorry this happened to you. Get over it because it's too upsetting for me.”

An old friend who isn’t a mother told me she knew just how I felt because her husband lost his son to suicide (someone she didn’t give birth to and didn’t know for very long).

Two years after Keven’s death, an acquaintance mentioned, “Well, you knew he'd die; you said so yourself.” So, yes, my greatest fear came true, but being reminded didn’t help.

One of my friends once compared his three kids, who all went to college, to my dead son. He said he and his wife “Raised our kids right,” implying it was my fault that Keven turned to drugs, had a mental illness, and took his own life. I was shocked into silence and did not respond other than to say, "Well, it was nice to see you," and I walked away.

Grief and loss are difficult topics to discuss but shouldn't be. Grief is a natural part of life when we lose someone or something we love. Besides death, it happens when we lose our jobs, our marriages, our health, our relationships, and of course, our pets. Unfortunately, we often rely on clichés like:

"He's in a better place now."
"Let me know what I can do for you."
"You're still young; you'll find another spouse in time."
"That job wasn't right for you; you'll get a better one."

Platitudes rarely provide comfort. We think bringing up the loss will upset the griever more. Grieving people are already thinking about their loss every day. Avoiding the topic makes grievers wonder if you've forgotten or don't care about what they are going through.

Losing someone suddenly, or when expected, differs in some ways, but the grief is the same. As uncomfortable as it may be, reach out to the grieving person to let them know you care. Don't have any expectations. Everyone handles grief in their own way. It's better to say something than nothing, even if it's just a few words.

Witnessing grief is uncomfortable; it can be emotional and frustrating. Families and friends will feel more confident and comfortable supporting someone when they understand what grieving feels like. You'd like to help, but you don't know how. Do they want to be alone? Do they need company? Feel free to ask, and don't take their response personally; they might seem harsh, despondent, or too overwhelmed to know what they want. Checking on them often, especially in the beginning, is helpful. Continuing to check in with them as time goes on is invaluable.

Even if the tears have dried up, we'll never stop missing those we've lost.

HOPE FOR THE GRIEVER

Your life has changed forever, and you may feel lost and alone. Many of us have ideas about what grief should be like, but it's different when it happens to us. Whatever you're feeling is legitimate; it's *your* grief. Listen to your gut and allow yourself to feel whatever comes up; don't let anyone tell you what you should or should not be feeling. We're unique individuals with different ways of handling life and death.

I don't believe time heals all wounds, but as with anything, we get better at it as time passes. We learn to live with our loss. As the days and weeks go by, the grief gets less overwhelming. You might feel debilitated initially, but you'll return to your old routines. The pain and sadness don't leave but become more bearable.

Share with your family and friends what would help you and what kind of support you need. One of the reasons I wrote this book is because you might not know what you need. Your brain is going through physical changes because of your loss. There's a name for this fogginess and inability to think clearly. It's called "grief brain." You'll learn more about that in the next chapter.

You will get through this. It won't be easy. Support groups and friends who care are essential to the process.

CHAPTER 4

GRIEF BRAIN IS REAL

Sometimes when hanging out with other grieving moms, one of us will forget something, and we will all chime in and say, “Grief brain!” It's done in a fun way because we can all relate to it, but there's nothing funny about how frustrating it is.

You get grief brain when your brain's neurochemicals and hormones are disrupted, causing these symptoms:

- Forgetfullness
- Clumsiness
- Anxiety
- Irritability
- Being easily overwhelmed
- Trouble staying focused
- Brain Fog

“Grief Brain” was coined by Erich Lindemann in the 1940s. Lindemann was a psychiatrist who studied grief. He did research with the grieving survivors of the Coconut Grove tragedy (a nightclub fire in Chicago that took the lives of 492 people).[1]

When faced with a traumatic loss, our brain gets scrambled with different hormones, and it's hard to think straight. This is how Neurologist Lisa M. Shulman MD, FAAN, explains The Brain's Response to Grief:

Grief comes in many forms. Whether brought on by the death of a loved one, a serious illness or injury, divorce, abuse, or another cause, the brain interprets grief as emotional trauma.

> We perceive traumatic loss as a threat to survival and default to protective survival and defense mechanisms." This response engages the fight-or-flight mechanism, which increases blood pressure and heart rate and releases specific hormones. Grief and loss affect the brain and body in different ways. They can cause changes in memory, behavior, sleep, and body function, affecting the immune system and the heart. It can also lead to cognitive effects, such as brain fog. The brain's goal? Survival.[2]

Here is my definition of Grief Brain: The lack of ability to remember what you know, constantly forgetting things, feeling like you're losing your mind, and inability to recall names, places, and memories.

Have you ever run into an acquaintance and wracked your brain trying to remember their name and how you know them? It's common. With Grief Brain, that can happen when you run into someone you know well. It's very embarrassing.

Sometimes I could not remember what I did the previous day. On several occasions, I couldn't remember my social security number or had to stop and think hard before stating my address. I've never been known for having a great sense of direction, but I would find myself lost on the streets of a city I've lived in for fifty years.

Sometimes I'd be in a conversation and couldn't make sense of what the other person was saying. I'd get lost in my thoughts, wondering, *should I tell them I have no clue what they just said, or should I fake like I know?* Or I'd be talking and completely lose my train of thought mid-sentence.

Grief Brain kept me from looking for a job. I needed one after I lost Kev but felt incapable of learning something new. If I'd had an old job to go back to, I would have been okay in time, but two and a half years ago, learning something new wasn't realistic.

Sometimes we're used to seeing our friends and loved ones in a certain way, then grief hits, and they display emotions or behaviors that are completely out of character for what we're used to.

Grief Brain falls into that category. Be gentle with those who are grieving, and be prepared to assist them with difficult decisions or tasks if they seem overwhelmed. You can help them find the answer if you know it (like where something is in the house, the month/date, or what needs to be done next.)

HOPE FOR THE GRIEVER

It's not your fault you can't think straight. It gets better. Like everything in grief, the strong physical and emotional reactions that occur in the beginning, including your brain functions, will slowly fade. Be patient with yourself; it happens to most of us. It's natural and to be expected. Explain it to your family and friends if they're worried you're "losing it," and have them do a Google search for "Grief Brain." Chances are they haven't heard of it unless they've experienced it themselves.

---

1. Grief: A Brief History of Research on How Body, Mind, and Brain Adapt - PMC (nih.gov) Mary-Frances O'Connor, PhD
2. The Healing Power of Grief, with Dr. Lisa Shulman - This Is Your Brain

CHAPTER 5

GRIEF IS PART OF LIFE NOT A DISORDER

If asked for a grief book recommendation, I always recommend *It's Okay Not to Be Okay* by Megan Devine. The title of the book says it all. She talks about how we all grieve differently and reminds us that grief has no expiration date. This makes sense to me since we're all individuals with unique situations. But unfortunately, society sees grief as something negative, something to "get over."

In March 2022, I discovered that the DSM-5 added a new disorder to their reference book: [1]"Prolonged Grief Disorder." My thoughts on this: *What!?*

If you are unfamiliar with the DSM, it stands for Diagnostic and Statistical Manual of Mental Disorders (currently in Edition 5). It's the American Psychiatric Association's "bible" for diagnosing mental illness.

People shouldn't tell another person their grief is a disorder because it doesn't end in *their* designated timeframe. I'm not the only one who thinks this. Clinical psychologist Noël Hunter, PsyD, who specializes in trauma and grief, calls it abysmal and reprehensible. She posits:

> This is yet another disgusting display of overreach, pharmaceutical influence, and an inability as a society to tolerate painful emotions. The updates to the DSM are, sadly, representative of a process that has been troubled from the start.

Grief is a normal human emotion, but if our culture calls it a disorder, we feel like there's something wrong with us—there isn't. After a loved one dies, it's natural to be sad, lonely, heartbroken, depressed, and unable to focus. You can't imagine enjoying life again in the early stages of grief. Feelings will slowly improve, but we can't rush it. When you lose a spouse or a child, it's life-changing and forever. Here are some words describing how someone might feel after losing a loved one:

- Angry
- Depressed
- Despondent
- Devastated
- Distressed
- Heartbroken
- Hopeless
- In pain
- Lost
- Miserable
- Mournful
- Sad
- Suffering
- Tormented
- Tortured
- Useless

Maybe you've experienced some of these. I've felt all these things since losing Keven and Anthony. Although no one wants to experience any of these emotions, losing someone who has been an important part of your life changes everything.

Studies show letting our emotions out helps us heal. Holding them in or masking them, like I did with my dad's death, eats away at us like an infection. Eventually, the emotions will surface and explode. We can avoid debilitating breakdowns by expressing our emotions through therapy, crying, journaling, or talking with others who understand. Our emotions in grief will be easier to deal with when we feel them purposefully.

It might surprise you to hear I don't want to get over my grief. It makes sense if we think of grief as love. The deeper you love, the harder you grieve. I'll never stop missing Keven and Anthony and wishing they were still with me. To cope, I respond immediately when the feelings surface. This can mean crying, screaming, or writing a letter to one of them. Naturally, if I'm out in public, I don't scream, but I may cry. My grief does not control me if I express it. My life still has joy, laughter, and purpose, but it takes practice. Some days are harder than others. But, we slowly learn to live within it.

Instead of trying to talk someone out of their grief, be by their side as they feel it. Allowing someone a safe space to express themselves is a valuable gift.

HOPE FOR THE GRIEVER

Grief is a normal response. It has a beginning but no end. It morphs along the way, and we learn to live within it. Most importantly, there is no right or wrong way to grieve. Whatever you're feeling is okay. However, expressing our emotions as they surface helps us cope.

Don't let the thought of grief never-ending discourage you

—the pain lessens, and you will learn to love, laugh and live your life again. The timing is different for everyone, and early grief is by far the most painful. So be gentle with yourself; it takes time.

---

1. Prolonged Grief Disorder: DSM-5 Updates Explained (verywellmind.com)

CHAPTER 6

GRIEF—EARLY & FOREVER

I think of grief as split into two phases: early grief and forever grief. There is a significant difference between grief in the first days, months, and years and grief after a significant amount of time. Everything is more difficult in early grief.

It has been forty-eight years since I lost my dad. I get sad whenever I think about everything he missed and how different my life and Keven's would have been if he were still here. It doesn't impact my life every day, though I still miss him a lot.

It's been eight years since I lost my mom. Every day I think of her, and sometimes I feel sad about her passing, but most of the time, I think of happy memories. She was the heart and soul of our family, and our family gatherings have never been the same. Most of us experience the loss of a parent at some point in our lives. Depending on how close we were to them makes a big difference in how much and how long we grieve.

As of this writing, Keven has been gone for two years and five months. My grief over his death is still fresh, but I feel myself adjusting to it as time moves on. I'll miss him every day for the rest of my life. However, it is no longer a daily occurrence for me to cry. One of the hardest parts is remembering all he went through in his last months, so I try not to dwell on it. The influence of Keven's death infuses my life, choices, and outlook. I'll never get over losing him. He's still a big part of my life, just not physically. I still talk to him; I feel his presence a lot. I think of this book and my previous one, *Keven's Choice*, as a tribute to him—he helped me find my purpose—reaching out to others to offer support and hope.

My first few days of grief were hell. There was a feeling of being outside of myself while experiencing the deepest pain I've ever felt. The first few weeks weren't much better. I write about it in my memoir, *Keven's Choice*. Here's an excerpt:

> As I walked into the grocery store the first time, I took my usual left turn down aisle four and stopped in front of the Rockstar energy drinks. I reached for one of the yellow cans, and it knocked the wind out of me. I would never need to buy these again. Keven was gone. Keven was not coming back. I began crying right there. Every aisle had something I would never buy again: blueberry pop tarts, green apples, lemonade, and ketchup. I grieved down every aisle.

Throughout the first year, I cried several times a day. I wrote my first book shortly after his death, and it helped me in two ways: first, it helped me process my feelings, and second, it became a passion project that filled my mind.

Friends and family will tell you to take care of yourself and to be careful driving and doing tasks. They are right; you need to pay extra attention at first. I ran a red light a few months after Keven died, something I'd never done before. I had to focus more in the kitchen for fear of accidentally chopping off a finger.

Year two was different. For me, the pain was still there, but not as raw. The sense of missing him was much greater—it had been over a year since I talked to him, touched him, or was around him.

The first year, everything reminded me of him. Leaving the house was painful because every street, every store, all the memories would rush in, and I would be overwhelmed with sadness. The second year wasn't as traumatic. Now, in the third year, it doesn't happen as close to home as much—only in other cities (where he'd been in rehab, arrested, etc.) Some of his favorite songs hurt less to hear now, but others will always sting because they remind me of his desperation.

After a year, I noticed many people had moved on, and few seemed to realize I was living on a different plane: a grieving mother. My closest friends and Solace for Hope recognize I'm not the same person. There have been some positive changes, too. Now, I do things I would have never done before (like writing this book and speaking in front of large groups of people).

Currently, this is the fourth month of year three. I see more of my old self realigning with the new me. Reaching out to other parents helps; we're each other's biggest supporters because we're in the same boat. As I write this book, I have something to focus on. If it weren't a book, I'd have to find something else meaningful to do. Those are the things that keep me going.

Early grief hurts more. Supporting someone in early grief is like giving them a lifeline when they feel like they're drowning.

HOPE FOR THE GRIEVER

In the early stages of grief, you may look the same on the outside, but feelings of grief have hijacked your mind and emotions. Each of us will find our way to move forward after early grief. Finding others with a loss like yours can be a tremendous comfort. They understand what you're going through, which helps because they know firsthand how much it hurts.

It will become more bearable as time passes, and you'll feel better. When it seems like you won't be able to handle it anymore, remember it will get better.

CHAPTER 7

PROCESSING GRIEF

There are a lot of resources out there about processing grief. It's easy to find articles and books about specific types of grief. Many books tell you there's a way to get over grief and lay out a plan. Here's the thing, even though some of this advice is good and helpful, it doesn't make grief any easier to process.

Early grief makes it hard to get out of bed, pick up the phone, or walk to the mailbox—adding "guidelines for healing" is overwhelming. The wounds are still wide open; they need to close a bit for healing to begin. It's important to be patient with yourself and let go of expectations.

Grievers can expect to be triggered in the early days, weeks, and months. Triggers can pop up every day, anywhere. I couldn’t drive down a street without memories of Keven or Anthony rushing in. Familiar songs, smells, places, things, and people all had the potential to trigger tears. Anniversaries, holidays, special occasions, or traditions will remind you of your loved one. Those days are some of the most challenging to navigate.

I experienced a trigger as I sat in the same courtroom where Keven and Anthony saw each other for the last time. Keven was in custody after being arrested for possession of a controlled substance, so he was in the glass "cage" with all the other inmates. Anthony had a court appearance for something drug-related. As it turned out, they were both appearing before the same judge at the same time; I accompanied Anthony partly so I could see Keven, too; just getting a glimpse of him was worth it. Court rules are stringent, and waving or motioning to someone in custody is forbidden. But that didn't stop Anthony from giving Keven the heart/I love you sign with his hands. Keven returned the gesture. That was their last communication ever.

Memories aren't as intense as triggers. We can't control when or where a memory will pop up, but we can control how we handle it. I tend to push away painful memories; there's no point in remembering Keven's worst moments. It's something I know in my heart, so I don't dwell on it. As soon as I notice my mind going to that dark place, I force myself to change my thoughts and focus on something else.

Once again, everyone is different. One person may find going back to work the best way to cope. Others must take an extended leave because they aren't ready to face it. There is no right or wrong way to grieve.

SUGGESTIONS FOR PROCESSING GRIEF

Give yourself permission to feel whatever comes up without fighting it. It's all okay. There are so many emotions you might go through. One minute you're smiling at a happy memory, and the next, you're crying because you miss them. If you need to identify your feelings, journal or find someone willing to listen and let it all out. It's okay to take a break from your thoughts. Watch a movie, read, nap, run, and do what works for you. There were many times when I wanted to step out of my body and leave the grief behind. That would have been great if it worked, but it didn't. So even though grief feels like it might kill us, it won't.

Share your experience with someone else. For me, it's easier to talk to someone who's experienced a loss like mine. They understand the depth of sadness. Friends and family can only imagine our despair—other parents who've lost a child can feel it. Plus, people feel uncomfortable talking about it with me. I can see it in their eyes. The value of support groups for specific types of loss (spouse, child, overdose, etc.) is huge. You might meet a few people who become close friends. I have, and they're priceless.

Remember, this is *your* grieving process. No two people grieve the same. Let someone else's expectations go in one ear and out the other to save yourself from feeling angry or hurt. There's no way they'll understand what you're going through, but hopefully, they'll read this book and get an idea. I wrote it for that reason. I've heard people get upset after reading articles about how it "should" be, what works and what doesn't, and what timelines are for grief. Whatever you choose to do or not do is right for you. No one, including me, knows what's best for you. I've learned this, but please take what you like and leave what you don't.

Journal/write. Some people like to write; others don't. Try writing out your thoughts and feelings; if it doesn't work, don't force yourself. What I find helpful is writing letters to Keven and Anthony. I keep them up to date on what's going on in the world and my life. Mostly, I tell them how much I miss them and share wonderful memories. It felt weird at first, but now it feels peaceful. I used to write similar letters to each of them when they were in jail or prison.

Take care of yourself. If we only had a dollar for every time someone said that. It's natural for people who care to remind us how important it is to get enough sleep, eat enough, drink enough water, get outside in fresh air and sunshine, etc. Here I am, another one of those people saying the same thing. But don't beat yourself up if you can't force yourself off the couch, into the shower, or out the door in the beginning. In the first month of grief, I went two weeks without washing my hair (except for the day of Keven's memorial service). The thought of it overwhelmed me, but even more so, I didn't care about much of anything in those first few weeks. Nothing mattered anymore. But this feeling eventually passed, and it will for you too. Go at your own pace. Be gentle and kind to yourself. You have the rest of your life to get back to healthy habits. In early grief, just getting through a day may be all you can handle. In forever grief, these things will be part of your day-to-day routine again.

Let people know what you need. This is difficult for most of us. I was raised to keep my feelings and thoughts to myself and never burden anyone. It took me half my life to learn how to communicate my needs. Some of us can read minds; however, most of us can't. It's especially hard for those of us who are afraid of saying or doing the wrong thing. Sometimes we don't know what we need. I hope some of what I share in this book will help friends and loved ones of grievers. That's what Part Three of this book is all about.

Read books. Before I wrote this book, I searched Amazon for books about grief. There are tons. Full disclaimer, I almost changed my mind. I kept asking myself, *does the world need one more book on grief?* However, my writer friends encouraged me to keep going because, yes, there are a ton of books, but we're all different. Some may resonate with us; some won't. I hope mine resonates with you. If not, please start with *It's Okay Not to Be Okay* by Megan Devine and go from there.

Listen to podcasts. There are an overwhelming number of podcasts out there. My suggestion is to search for one using very specific criteria: grieving the loss of a friend who died of cancer, grieving the loss of an ex-spouse, grieving the loss of a sibling, a suicide, an accidental death, etc. Focus your search on your specific situation and needs. Maybe reading or hearing about grief is the last thing you want—plenty of fiction books and interesting podcasts can be a temporary distraction.

Memorialize your loved one. My friends Rodger and Kim dedicated a space in their backyard to a memorial garden for their son, Riley. It's beautiful! There are plants, photos, garden art, and special reminders of their precious son. Some people have a park bench dedicated to their loved ones, plant a tree, create a space in their home for photos and candles, or an urn. I have a few little spots in my home dedicated to Keven. The main one is his place at the kitchen table. His urn is there, and it's "wearing" one of his favorite fedoras. Next to it are candles, photos, and a square jar that holds his wallet, watch, glasses, and other odds and ends that were important to him. I have some of Anthony's ashes held by a large ceramic angel and some sitting on a shelf above our TV (the rest are buried with his mother).

Consider seeking professional help. There are therapists who specialize in grief. It's benefited many people who need a safe and trained person to share their feelings. I didn't choose this for myself, but I know people who have benefited from it. The resources at the back of the book have some suggestions.

You don't have to grieve alone. If I could make only one suggestion to help a grieving person, it would be to find a support group. There are so many benefits to being understood, and you realize a lot of what you're feeling is common. I talk to the people I've met through Solace for Hope about Keven and Anthony. They get it. They're always willing to listen or cry with me, even if they're struggling, too. In our darkest moments, acknowledging someone's pain with a hug or a kind word makes us feel better. With the Solace for Hope group, it's not all tears and sadness. We also laugh, socialize, and share special occasions. I list a few resources at the back of the book so you can check them out.

HOPE FOR THE GRIEVER

Don't have expectations about how your grief is progressing. It may be like a roller coaster of emotions. Test out some suggestions in this chapter and see what helps. Finding others experiencing the same type of grief can bring comfort and support.

Time doesn't heal wounds of loss, but time helps us live within them. Fighting it or trying to fit it in a neat little package prolongs the healing. We'll never get over it—our wounds will turn into a scar for us to see every day. But the original pain does become bearable.

CHAPTER 8

GRIEVING OUR OLD SELVES & ACCEPTING OUR NEW NORMAL

When someone you love passes on, you face the challenge of learning to live without them. Our lives change forever. Sometimes we grieve not only the person we lost but also the life we lived. We're starting a new chapter and finding our "new normal." The closer the person was to us, the more dramatic the changes.

So often, when listening to someone share their loss, I hear comments like, "My life changed at that moment" or "I haven't been the same since he/she died." Keep in mind this is a normal reaction. It may take months to recognize you've changed. It's not all negative. I have a new purpose in life that gives me motivation and satisfaction. I want to reach out to other hurting people, and there are many ways to do this; writing a book is just one of them. There are online groups full of compassionate people who can comfort you, or you can give comfort when you're ready. I volunteer for TIP (Traumatic Intervention Program) because it allows me to use my compassion and satisfies me knowing I've helped someone else (see resources for more information on TIP).

The most significant change for me after losing Keven was how obvious it became as to what really matters in life. There are so many things that don't matter—things that aren't worth getting upset over (traffic, mean people, being overweight, losing a physical object, the list is never-ending). For example, I rarely get impatient anymore. Many day-to-day annoyances no longer affect me. What really matters became clear after my loss.

So, what matters? People. People make up our lives, those we know, those we see around us, those around the globe. Being kind and helpful to others makes me feel good. If I can do that, I'm satisfied. It sounds so simple to say it out loud, but that's my perspective on life now.

Before losing Keven and Anthony, my life was focused on trying to save them. I spent years attempting to do the impossible. Love doesn't save lives, but I'd like to think knowing someone had their back, valued them, and loved them unconditionally helped ease some of their pain.

If you've been in a relationship, becoming single might be your new normal. Losing a spouse or partner must be one of the most difficult losses—I can only imagine how it feels. Losing your best friend, lover, co-parent, travel companion, financial provider/partner all at once. Suddenly, life turns upside down, and you have to figure out how to put it back together.

If you had only one child, you are suddenly no longer a parent (at least in the physical sense, we will always be our child's parent even when they're no longer with us). Losing a sibling or best friend leaves you without a confidant whom you shared all your secrets with, who knew you so well words were sometimes unnecessary. No one wants a new normal that involves a loss of these magnitudes.

In my case, after losing my son, our home was so quiet.

Without Keven, Therese, my sister, and I both had to adjust to seeing his empty chair and bedroom. There was less laughter in the house but also less stress and worry. It was boring without him around. There were stark reminders in every room, reminding us he was missing. There was less food in the fridge, less conversation, less teasing and jokes, and nagging and worry. My phone didn't ring as often. I didn't hear the familiar "Hey, Mom!" or "Mom?" or "I love you, Mom," which was my normal for twenty-nine years. I hate those parts of my *new normal.*

There are things you did and places you went with your loved one that may cause pain where they once brought joy. Traditions the two of you shared are permanently over. It's depressing and lonely, and different. Our old selves shift into our new selves—we discover our new normal whether we like it or not.

Maybe you can go back to the old traditions or places, maybe not. It's up to you and how you want to move forward. I don't think forcing yourself to do something that triggers you is helpful, but there are some occasions (family gatherings, holidays, events) where you'll want to show up. As I write this, it's Christmas Day 2022. I don't want to see anyone today. I'd rather stay home and pretend it's not a holiday. But I will go to my brother's house and do my best to get through the day.

There may be a temporary change in your behavior. You may respond differently to others than you did before. You may be disorganized and forgetful—more symptoms of grief brain. It lessens as time goes on, but I'm not sure if it ever completely goes away. I've always been super organized in all areas of my life; now, I'm forgetful, lose things, and often can't find things. It's very frustrating. Nowadays, it's hard for me to differentiate between grief brain and common forgetfulness.

You may have less interest in things that were once important to you. It surprised me I didn't lose interest in NHL hockey or live music in the first year after Keven's death. I felt guilty that I still cared if my Anaheim Ducks won or lost (what difference did it make? My son was dead; how trivial and insulting to care about a sport.) But it was helpful. It showed me even though my life had changed, parts of me were still there. Watching games or going out to hear music gave me hope there would be enjoyment in my life again (especially if the Ducks won).

Some patterns may change, including sleep, appetite, sexual interest, and exercise. It's easier to get run down or look haggard during early grief, which may bother you or may not. Stress, depression, and anxiety may become part of your new normal in the beginning. I've read grief can make you more prone to injury or illness. In the last two and a half years, I've hurt myself more often than before.

Quite a few moms I know asked their doctor to prescribe something to help take the edge off the worst moments. I didn't choose this path because I feared I'd become dependent. It's a personal decision to discuss with your doctor. There is no shame in seeking help through medication if you remain under the supervision of a physician who will taper you off the meds when the time is right.

Thankfully, there is hope—your new normal has some positive elements. It's not all darkness and sorrow once early grief fades. Before I lost Keven, I never would have considered doing the things I am doing now. I'd always wanted to write a book. I never had the guts to be vulnerable and put my words into the world.

After losing my boy, I discovered I no longer cared as much about what people thought of me, which freed me up to write *Keven's Choice*. Before, I cared too much about what people thought about me or my writing.

I am also much bolder about speaking out about things that matter to me, especially the stigma surrounding mental illness, substance use disorder, and suicide loss. I'm passionate about speaking up for medically assisted treatment for addicts, harm reduction, and treatment availability. I've been honored to be on quite a few podcasts and once (so far) have read from my book aloud in front of a group. These things are the exact opposite of the old me.

Everyone's new normal will be different. A griever's purpose doesn't have to be starting an organization, writing a book, or donating to worthy causes; it can be as simple as making someone smile. Recently, I heard about a grieving mom who hid money around a grocery store on the lower shelves (where the least expensive items and less fortunate families often buy from). She included a note that said something like, "Please accept this as an act of kindness." A few times, she was there when the money was found and saw the surprise and thankfulness on the recipient's face.

There are many creative ways to make ourselves feel purposeful that don't involve money. For example, just opening a door for someone while smiling is an act of kindness.

Finally, losing a loved one makes you think about your own mortality. We'll all experience it eventually. It's one of the few inevitable things in life. All we can do is take care of our health and live in a way that keeps us safe from harm. The rest is out of our control. Healthy people get sick and die; safe people have accidents. All we have is today. Finding things to be grateful for helps me when I dread the unknown.

HOPE FOR THE GRIEVER

Our old selves may be gone, but who we become because of our loss may surprise us in good ways. Just let your new normal unfold without expectations, positive or negative. After losing a loved one, we sometimes feel like giving up, but we keep going and find out how strong we are despite all our challenges. Don't underestimate the power of being kind to others. Let's help each other through this together.

CHAPTER 9

About Guilt & Regret

In grief, we need to deal with guilt and regret. When you lose someone, it's common to feel that way. Getting over my guilt and regret didn't happen naturally or immediately, but knowing it was on the horizon helped.

A feeling of guilt comes from doing something you know is wrong, while a feeling of regret comes from wishing you had done something different. Both feelings can surface, especially with a loss to substance use or suicide.

Feeling guilty doesn’t mean you are. Dissecting every encounter with our loved one and finding fault with our actions does nothing to help; we may become despondent or angry because of it. People usually respond by saying, “You shouldn’t feel that way; it wasn’t your fault.” Though it's true, grief isn't logical. If guilt continues to haunt you after your loss, talk to a friend or a therapist. No need to add guilt to what we already must deal with. We all make mistakes, and unfortunately, we can't go back and change them. If guilt surfaces, take a deep breath and try to let it go.

Regret is different. I've known people who beat themselves

up about things they wish they'd done differently, words they should have said or avoided. Though self-doubt and self-anger are understandable, they don't serve any useful purpose and make it hard to move forward. The past won't change. You might have made a difference with what you said or did, or maybe you wouldn't have. But, if we catch ourselves regretting the past, we can stop it in its tracks and refocus on something else.

After losing Keven and Anthony, I felt both guilt and regret. I had to let it go before it consumed me. I was legitimately guilty of failing to lock up my firearm, the handgun Kev used to end his life. Whenever it crept into my mind, I had to force it out. Whenever I caught myself going down that rabbit hole, I reminded myself he'd told me for years this was how his life would end; my gun wasn't the deciding factor. I remember the hug we shared that morning, telling each other we loved each other. Over and over, I'd remind myself that my mistakes as a parent came from a place of love. I did everything possible to help him. I knew this but had to reinforce it often. I still struggle with this often.

In my relationship with Anthony, I had regret but no guilt. If I hadn't bailed him out of jail when he got arrested in Colorado, he wouldn't have had to travel back for his court date. If he hadn't had to drive far, the girl who left him in the car to die wouldn't have been with him. I regretted putting him in that position. But, again, I had to let go of this. In the weeks following his death, it haunted me and made me feel sick. After journaling about it for hours, I let it go, but I had to get it out of my system first. Here's an excerpt of what I wrote:

Why the hell did I have to break my rule to

"never bail them out"?!?! If I'd left Anthony in jail in Colorado, he could have done his sentence and been over with it, but no, I had to feel sorry for him this time, so it's my fault he had to drive up there for court. It's all my fault!!! He's dead because I bailed him out!

Okay, Bar—seriously? Do you really, sincerely believe it's your fault he's dead? He may have hooked up with this girl even if he wasn't driving through Vegas to Colorado. He may have brought a different person along and still ended up dead. Did you do what you thought was best for him at the time? Then knock it off and stop blaming yourself. It's not your fault. Anthony would be so pissed off if he knew you were blaming yourself.

Recently I met a woman who blamed herself for her husband's death because she could not get him to go to the doctor for seven years. He'd been hospitalized for a stroke but refused any follow-up care and chose never to go to another medical appointment. He died of cardiac arrest, and this sweet woman was distraught, saying she had failed him. We had a good talk about it, and I hope I convinced her that he chose to ignore his health; she did all she could.

Acknowledging guilt and regret is the first step in letting go of guilt and regret. Consider the specific things that keep coming to mind. Getting them out of your head and onto paper is an excellent way to eliminate them. If you catch yourself returning to those thoughts, gently remind yourself to let them go. When I speak with someone carrying a heavy load of guilt and/or regret after a loss, I ask them, "Did you love the person? Did they know you loved them? Then that's all that matters."

HOPE FOR THE GRIEVER

Guilt and regret are normal and common parts of grief. Acknowledge them as they surface or attempt to write specifics. Do your best to let go, and then, when they creep back into your mind, redirect your thoughts by reminding yourself your person knew you loved them, and that's what matters. When you can let go of guilt and regret, you will feel lighter and less of a burden on your already heavy shoulders.

CHAPTER 10
SIGNS FROM OUR LOVED ONES

The signs I get from my mom, Keven, and Anthony bring me joy and comfort. Often, they make me laugh. However, the topic of signs from the dead is tricky since not everyone believes in them, and those who do sometimes get discouraged because they're looking for more frequent or obvious signs.

Some people see signs from common things like butterflies after the death of a loved one. On the one hand, we can argue butterflies aren't a sign, but who's to say they aren't? For me, Keven's signs are usually obvious, like when the radio turns on by itself and then turns off after playing the song "Knocking on Heaven's Door" (Guns N' Roses version). This sort of thing doesn't happen regularly, but once every few months, Therese or I will get some strange electronic sign from him.

I wanted more signs more often, so I created one. Where I live, ground squirrels are popular, but tree squirrels are rare. Years ago, when Keven was still here, a tree squirrel showed up in our yard and started hanging around occasionally. Keven loved squirrels and used to feed several by hand, so he was excited to have this unusual visitor. Sometimes we wouldn't see the squirrel for a year, but he always returned.

After Keven left us, the squirrel started showing up regularly, and we named him "Blaze," a self-titled nickname Kev gave himself as a young child. Blaze may disappear for a week or a month—but unlike when Kev was here, he's never been gone longer than that. Therese and I (and the dogs!) get excited each time he (she?) shows up in the yard. I occasionally put out peanuts for our friend, the more sightings, the better.

Is it really a sign from Keven when Blaze shows up? Doubtfully, but what's the harm in thinking it is? It brings me great joy regardless of whether it is true. It makes sense because of Keven's love of squirrels; I see no harm in it. I need all the happiness I can get.

For those of you who don't believe in signs, let those of us who do enjoy ours. If you're feeling ripped off or envious that your friends always see signs and you don't, try using your imagination. Although we want our signs to be real, we may miss some of them; there is no harm in creating our own idea of what our loved one uses as a sign that they are near.

Universally thought of signs from the deceased:

Feathers. Feathers on the ground mean you are not alone.
Hearts. This symbol of love is popular. They can be found anywhere. I think the hearts found in nature are beautiful signs (rocks, shadows, the shape of a leaf or cloud).
Dragonflies. They carry spiritual messages.
Repeating numbers. It could be a sign if you associate a certain number with your loved one and see it often.
Specific timing or validations. Your loved one may try to get

your attention or send you a message through "coincidental" timing of something or validation you're that on the right path.

Songs. You turn on some music, and the song that is playing reminds you of a loved one, or you're talking or thinking about them in a public place, and one of their songs comes on (this happens to me at the grocery store sometimes).

Dreams. Having someone you love and miss show up in a dream can be a sign.

Finding coins. When you find money on the ground, pick it up and look at the date. It could be a number significant to your loved one.

Hearing their voice in your head. I love it when this happens. In fact, I just heard it. When I hear Keven or Anthony's voices, it's "I love you," "Mom," or the sound of their laughter.

Lights or electronics going on and off. This one is both cool and annoying. Lights flickering is cool; the TV going off right when the Anaheim Ducks are about to score a goal is annoying. This has happened occasionally; it always comes right back on.

Scents that remind you of your loved one. My favorite scent is Aqua Di Gio mixed with Marlboro Smooths (Keven) and the scent of Anthony's favorite lotion (Vaseline Intensive Care).

An endless list of things can be thought of as signs. Try to have an open mind. Let it be fun rather than hyper-focusing on seeing them often or having them be too obvious.

HOPE FOR THE GRIEVER

Some of us receive signs all the time, others not so often or not at all. What are your personal beliefs on signs being sent from beyond? There's nothing wrong with making up something to be your sign from someone you lost. Try giving yourself permission to make up a special sign and see if it brings you joy.

PART THREE

DIFFERENT TYPES OF LOSS

CHAPTER 11

LOSS OF A CHILD

It's often said that losing a child is the greatest loss there is. It doesn't matter how many kids you have, losing one is one too many. With more than one child, parents also suffer watching their surviving children grieve. It doesn't matter how old the child was, a newborn or an adult. It doesn't matter if the child is fully formed or not. Any pregnancy that ends without a living baby is child loss. It's never "natural" to lose a child, so when it happens, it's tragic.

Without losing Keven, I wouldn't have seen the need for this book. I wouldn't know the suffering hundreds of thousands of parents go through. It's impossible to describe the agony of a parent who's lost a child. It's different from any other loss because our kids are part of us. Kids are supposed to be here when we leave, not the other way around. Mothers and fathers bring them into the world; they're supposed to stay with us until we're gone.

The following excerpt from my book, *Keven's Choice: A Mother's Journey Through Her Son's Mental Illness, Addiction and Suicide*, describes my early grief:

> It felt like part of him lingered around in those first days, especially in his room. The moment my hand turned the doorknob, my senses went into overdrive. His scent surrounded me like a warm embrace. I never wanted it to go away. Blood had covered his bed, so the cleaning crew removed it. His dirty clothes sat in one laundry basket and clean ones in another. I buried my face in his T-shirt, crying, knowing the scent would eventually fade.
>
> I looked the same from the outside, but waves of grief were tossing my inner self. It was hard to breathe. I had a literal pain in my chest. There was a heaviness to my movements. Everything around me was out of focus. I felt like I was suffocating. It felt as though the people in my life had forgotten about Keven and were unaware my life, as I knew it, was over. Those first months felt like I was living in a different dimension of reality.
>
> Going out to run my usual errands became a dreaded task because every clerk and cashier would ask the same innocent question: "How are you today?" followed by "Have a nice day!" I wished this nicety would go away. Do I tell the truth or lie? The few times I answered honestly, it created an awkward moment for everyone within earshot.
>
> Nothing was the same, not even the most straightforward social exchanges. It was apparent how ill-prepared our culture is to deal with grief.

People who haven't experienced child loss look at me differently. I imagine a parent who's lost a child to an illness or accident gets an immediate response of sympathy and compassion. However, when you talk about losing a child to an overdose or suicide, it's not always the same. Most people feel bad for me, but some judge Keven and me. They are uncomfortable around me. Not knowing what to say makes them not say anything, which hurts even more than saying the wrong thing. Or they say things to try and cheer me up; they give me unsolicited advice; they talk about the future too soon; they compare their grief experiences.

What did I want in those early days of grief? I wanted people to talk about my son. It didn't make me sad; I was already sad. It didn't remind me of my loss; the loss permeated my being. I wanted to hear happy memories from anyone who ever knew him. I let his friends know this; they brought me so much comfort in the beginning months. I wanted anyone who had a photo of him to send it to me. I wanted the world to know a precious person was no longer on earth.

I also wanted people to accept the new me and not minimize the loss by saying things like "time heals all wounds," "this will strengthen you," and "it was his time." I certainly didn't want to hear the familiar "suicide is selfish" or "Do you blame yourself?" comments and questions.

Age doesn't matter in child loss. My grandmother was in her 80s when she lost my father, one of the youngest of her nine children. She lived to be ninety-eight years old. He was the only child she lost, and she never got over it.

When a young parent loses a baby or has a miscarriage, please, please don't say something like, "You can have (or you have) more children," or "At least you didn't really know the baby," or "it wasn't a baby yet." You may as well say, "You shouldn't be grieving. Your baby doesn't matter."

Sometimes people express *extra* concern when they hear I lost my only child. They say things like, "How tragic to lose your *only* child!" When losing my only child, I also lost any future grandchildren, a daughter-in-law, a reason to celebrate the holidays, and someone to take care of me when I'm too old to do everything for myself. But it's no more tragic than losing *any* child, whether you have one or six. It doesn't matter how many children you have or how old they are, the one you lost is gone forever, and the grief is as great as the grief of a parent of an only child.

When parents have grandchildren by their lost child, it can be a comfort and joy to be around them, but it's also a reminder of what they're missing out on. It's okay to express your sadness to children in an age-appropriate way. It shows them it's okay to talk about missing their parent. Sometimes having grandchildren means putting on a cheerful face, especially on holidays. It's one of those things we learn to do. I can't specifically relate to having grandchildren, but I imagine it takes a toll to ignore the pain of missing your child while trying to keep things light for your grandchild.

Quite a few parents I know are raising their grandchildren in their child's absence (either by death or inability to parent). I admire them so much. People tell me, "You'd do the same if Keven left behind a kid," and I suppose I would, but it's got to be exhausting; it's a very selfless act to give up your "golden years" to raise another child/children.

Parents may feel guilty that they cannot be the same parent for their surviving children. It devastates them to see them suffering the loss of their sibling. Some parents try not to grieve too openly in front of their kids, and some parents cling to their surviving children or worry about them constantly.

This story, from my friend Laura Swank, leads us from child loss to sibling loss. I never knew her son, Harley, in life, but I feel I did because of all the beautiful memories and photos she shared. Laura's son, Harley Swank, passed away from a drug overdose in 2018. He was just nineteen years old at the time.

THOUGHTS FROM A MOM—LAURA SWANK

Life without Harley is heartbreaking, difficult, sad, emotional, scary, traumatic, lonely, life-changing, anxiety-producing, depressing, enlightening, evolving, spiritually seeking, and constantly learning, and I have a mission to help others that are struggling, which I didn't before because I was always trying to help save my boys.

For his older brother, it has been extremely difficult; It changed his life. He was suicidal for many years, and in such a deep dark hole, I didn't think he would make it out. After almost five years, he is finally emerging into life again. His depression, anxiety, and PTSD were something I had to deal with while dealing with my own grief; I put mine on hold to help him with his. Losing a child affects every aspect of your life.

What helped my grief journey was being told about a grief group through One Legacy (the Organ Donation Organization Harley's organs were donated.) From that group, I learned about other groups. Being able to speak freely about the loss of my child with other parents who had lost a child was and has been my salvation. Sharing my heart with other parents who understand the pain has comforted me the most.

I have surrounded myself with others that understand, and in my work life, I do not share my personal life, so very few exchanges have upset me. I am lucky my family has been understanding and has not pressured me or expected me to do or act a certain way. There have been no expectations, only understanding. I am one of the lucky ones. I know this to be true as I have heard many sad stories that are the opposite.

> I have learned a lot since my son died about grief and stigma. I'm sad it took my son's death to understand the meaning of empathy and meeting people where they are. I have regrets, but I know I did the best I could with the information I had at the time, and everything I did was out of love; I would do it all over again because to have loved with all my heart is the greatest gift.

Life goes on after child loss, but it's not the same. You live with an emptiness in your heart. Time will pass, and you'll be able to manage and enjoy parts of life again. Sunsets will be pretty again, and you can laugh; celebrations will be happy, and you might find joy in unexpected places. We all need a different amount of time; there's no standard timeline. There's a chance you'll discover something new about yourself that surprises you, like the courage to speak in front of a group, which I would've never done before. Other parents who've lost can be your greatest support, others want to help, but until you've been there, it's hard to fathom how devastating it is. Reach out; no one should have to go through this alone.

CHAPTER 12
LOSS OF A SIBLING

There's one thing a parent who's lost an only child doesn't have to deal with—the heartbreak of their other children. As Laura mentioned, her son became suicidal after his brother's death. Unfortunately, Harley's brother is not alone. Many siblings suffer from mental health issues after losing a brother or sister.

Siblings suffer a deep loss and often get overlooked because parents get all the attention. They're asked, "How are your parents doing with the loss?" instead of, "How are you doing with it?" This needs to be resolved. Siblings left behind see their parents and other family members grieving, and some feel they must be strong for them. Siblings often find themselves in limbo, trying to grieve and be supportive at the same time.

THOUGHTS FROM A SIBLING—ELLIE MARKES

> My big brother Toby died from a heroin overdose on July 22nd, 2021, just over a month after his 30th birthday. Unfortunately, we did not find out about his death until three days later because his roommates left him instead of calling the police. I'll never understand why his friends didn't think he was important enough to be helped, but I have to live with it.
>
> My brother started using heroin at fourteen years old and battled with this disease until his passing. What I admired most about my brother is that he never gave up, despite the odds against him. Toby was the kindest and most giving soul a sister could ask for. Despite what he was up against, my brother always tried to help me with my sobriety journey. He was my biggest cheerleader.
>
> It's been a painful and lonely journey since his passing. Addiction runs in my family, and my brother was the closest person in my life. Unfortunately, I've lost friends since his passing, and my family doesn't talk about his passing much, so I've found different ways to deal with my pain, like a grief group for family members who've lost a loved one to substance abuse/mental health issues and volunteering at recovery fundraisers in my area.
>
> Having struggled with substance abuse myself and watching my brother struggle, I've learned that you can't love someone enough to make them get sober. Toby would still be with me if he could.

Siblings are supposed to be together for a lifetime. Losing a brother or sister is one of the most painful losses, especially with a drug overdose or suicide—it feels so unfair. Sometimes they have guilt thinking they should have been able to help their sibling more, or they have survivor's guilt.

In a way, siblings lose their parents at the same time the sibling dies because mom and dad are not the same people after losing a child. We can't be—part of us is gone. Some siblings retreat, and others work hard to console their parents. It takes an enormous toll on them.

Some siblings are so profoundly affected by the loss of their brother or sister that they fall into a deep depression or develop a mental illness. I can think of four families I know that are dealing with this, so if there are four in my small circle, it must not be uncommon.

I know firsthand what it's like to watch a child suffer from mental illness—debilitating anxiety and depression, hearing voices, etc. When parents are in this situation, they feel grief plus fear, and helplessness.

So, no, it's not more devastating or difficult to lose an only child. It's devastating and difficult, no matter how many children you have. Bereaved parents aren't looking for comparisons or sympathy. We're just looking for acknowledgment that our lives are forever changed and hoping our family and friends will join us in keeping our missing child's memory alive.

As Ellie shared, losing a sibling you are exceptionally close to changes your life forever. The family dynamic is never the same without the missing sibling. You may find it healing to keep your sibling's memory alive by talking about them often, making a scrapbook of great memories, or finding your way of honoring their life. Finding others with a similar loss can help the healing process.

CHAPTER 13
LOSS OF A PARENT

As I write this, a close friend just lost his mother. He's seventy-one, and his mother was ninety-two. It's easy to think it won't be as hard because his mom was so old and lived a full life. She was "ready to go." But age doesn't matter when you lose one of your parents. Our parents were there for us our entire lives. They are the first ones to love us, to teach us, and to be there for us as we traverse through life—especially the rough patches. It's like losing the person who always had your back.

Not everyone has healthy, loving parents. That's also a type of grief. You are grieving the loss of what almost everyone around you had that you never experienced and may have longed for all your life. Losing the opportunity to reconcile is additional grief to bear. If you were the primary caregiver for your parent, their passing may be somewhat of a relief. Caregiving is emotionally and physically exhausting. It's natural to feel this relief. It has nothing to do with how much you loved or will miss them.

Losing a parent early in life can change your entire future.

As mentioned earlier, losing my dad at age fifteen sent me down a path I may have avoided if he were still alive. Children can grow up just fine with grandparents or other adults that love them as much as their parents, but when a parent dies, young kids can feel abandoned. It can cause them to fear losing the other parent.

When your second parent dies, it is natural to feel orphaned or abandoned. I was in my fifties when my mom passed. Realizing I no longer had a parent in my life caused me to feel vulnerable. There was no one "above me" in our immediate family. Fortunately, I still have a wonderful aunt who will be ninety-five soon. Her mind is still sharp, her heart full of love, and her body gets around great for someone her age.

Watching them reach old age and passing on reminds us we, too, will age and eventually leave our loved ones behind. It's the most natural loss there is, but that doesn't make it easier to grieve. It can be a very complex mix of emotions. The family loses a generation when the second parent/grandparent passes on.

Losing a parent often comes with the responsibility of handling their affairs. It can be a very busy and stressful time. Grief can be delayed due to all the business of arranging a service, dealing with the finances, etc. It may crash like a huge wave once all the details are taken care of. First, allow yourself to feel what you may have been suppressing to handle all the details. Then, give yourself time to rest.

Despite having my father in my life for only fifteen years, I am grateful to have had my mom for over fifty.

There are times when both parents die at the same time or very close together. My friend Paul Lesinski knows what this is like after losing his parents, John and Eleanor. Here is his story.

THOUGHTS FROM A SON—PAUL LESINSKI

I lost my dad on September 30, 2015. He was eighty-four years old. In 2003, he suffered a stroke that left him bedridden. As a result, his entire left side was immobilized, and his mind was also impacted. Although he could still talk and had his memories mostly intact, he was certainly a different person.

In 2014 he went to hospice due to heart failure. However, to all our amazement, he recovered. His caregiver said in twenty-seven years; she had never seen anyone come off hospice, at least someone in my dad's condition.

My dad's death was a gift. He needed to be free of his broken body. After he came off hospice in 2014, we felt like we had over a year of "extra" time, and I had made my peace with him about any issues we'd had in the past. I was fortunate in that sense. As he was taking his last breaths, I was able to be alone with him and tell him, "You were a great dad." Then my mom arrived, and the caregiver said she overheard her tell him, "I will see you soon." That was a gut punch, but she was right.

My mom died two and a half months later, at eighty-three. She developed a blood disorder called myelodysplastic syndrome, known as "pre-leukemia." She had undergone chemotherapy, plus blood transfusions, the previous year, which extended her time with us. But when she died, it came on very fast. We were all having dinner one week, and the next week, she was gone. Like my dad, her body shut down. My wife and I were there when she passed. I played "Blackbird" by the Beatles on guitar as she faded away with my wife holding her hand.

As beautiful as that sounds, I was devastated by her loss.

However, my mother's loss hit me differently than my father's death. She had been my dad's primary caregiver for many years longer than she should have been, and we had to force her into receiving help. My dad's health had been far too complicated for her to manage, but their generation was not very open to handing things like this off, even to far more qualified professionals. So, when my dad died, I had hoped my mom could have had a little freedom, maybe even travel a little. I wanted her to do some of the things she wasn't able to when she took care of my dad.

So, with her passing happening so soon after losing my dad, there were all sorts of feelings of unfairness and, of course, the usual grief when losing loved ones. If my dad's death was a gift, my mom's was a punch in the face. My mom left an indelible mark on family and friends through her service, strength, faith, and generosity.

My wife and I are practicing Catholics, and through our church and kids' school, we were blown away by the community's support. Meal trains, check-ins, we even had someone drop off a Christmas tree. One of my friends forced me into a local bar the night my mom died so we could have some drinks to toast her memory. It made a world of difference, and we have done the same thing as our friends who have lost loved ones.

Community plays a huge role in supporting and processing grief—sharing stories and talking about memories all helped. Even simple things like sending a text on the first birthday or holiday after the passing are helpful to check in.

No matter how old our parents are or how old we are when we lose them, it's a profound loss. After losing both parents, we can feel like "an orphan" because the person who shaped our lives is no longer here. If your relationship with your parent(s) was strained or even nonexistent, maybe you've already been grieving them for years—but it may still hurt when they pass on.

You can keep your parents' memory alive by ensuring all future generations know about them. Consider writing something that can be passed along or making a video that shares your fondest memories.

CHAPTER 14
LOSS OF A SPOUSE OR LIFE PARTNER

Having never been married, I'm unable to speak about what it would be like to lose a spouse or a significant other. I can only imagine all the emotions and changes that would occur. Margie Allman shares about her loss of Alfred, the love of her life.

THOUGHTS FROM A LIFE PARTNER—MARGIE ALLMAN

Like many couples who've been together for a couple of decades, we had our ups and downs. We'd been in a down-phase: him angry with me for devoting all my time and energy to training for an Ironman triathlon, me with him for not being supportive.

"Just let me do this," I wasn't asking. I was going across the country to compete, despite his asking me not to go. After eight months of training, surely, it was the right thing to do. To show up for me.

I'd seen the little accident that was, unbeknownst to

anyone, causing his slow death. How bad could it be? He'd been lying on the floor with that knobby, hard foam roller vertically underneath him. Pushing himself with his feet, he moved his body so the roller went up and down his back. A self-massage. Like he always did. Then, he rolled off the side of it and onto the floor. Like he always did. It had a thin, gold, metal rim around the end.

"Ow," he said, clutching his side. What could have happened? How was that day's rolling off different from all the other days? I figured it was a little case of 'man-sick'.

A week later, I left for the triathlon. A week after that, the day before I was coming home, he died. The autopsy said it was a punctured lung.

He had told me he felt like he was dying.

I sure as hell didn't have his back, like we'd had each other's so many times over the years. I didn't act like he was my best friend like I claimed. How could I have let him down like that?

I talked openly about his death. Maybe I was looking for assurance that I was not, in fact, a loveless asshole but a mere human who, in the face of a few unknowns, simply chose myself. It is still one of the most regrettable decisions of my life.

It's been eight years, and his spirit is clear, energetic, and with me often. Out of the blue, I hear his voice telling me it's okay. That it was a stupid accident. I've learned that I must forgive myself, even though, at times, I still feel unforgivable. Now and then, I get this sense of peace, a warmth, almost like an otherworldly embrace, and a feeling of being loved. I choose to believe this is him. It gives me the comfort I need to go on.

CHAPTER 15

LOSS OF A FRIEND

Grieving a friend doesn't get much attention compared to losing a child, parent, or spouse. Our friends are some of the most important, cherished people in our lives. Friends are chosen, unlike family, who we're stuck with, if we like it or not. All kidding aside, I'd be lost without my best friend, Kathy. She's been in my life for forty-eight years, so you can imagine how well we know each other. We've had our difficult moments, as all good friends do, but we both know we will always be there for each other, encouraging, listening, and sharing in sorrow and joy.

I've asked my friend Mike Duffy to share about his friend, Matt Krapf. Matt died of blood cancer at age forty-four, only two months after his diagnosis:

THOUGHTS FROM A FRIEND—MIKE DUFFY

Life without Matt is diminished in such important ways. I miss our daily talks and constant laughter. I miss talking with him about working on a car, a house, or a motorcycle. I miss talking about how much snow we got and the latest job misadventure. I miss talking about our families and our challenges as dads and husbands. I miss talking to him about everything in my life.

But most importantly, I lost a deep part of myself, a part of me that believed in me. I needed that voice desperately in the next few years, but it was no longer there. My eyes well up as I write this—I loved him like few others in my life.

What helped me most in my grief was time and keepsake memories. When I remember Matt, I feel I'm keeping his wonderful essence alive. The pictures of our motorcycle trip are wonderful, and I always keep a framed copy of the Beartooth pass picture close to me.

The best way people helped me with my grief was to celebrate his life. It was in sharing good and bad stories about who he was. It was connecting on how he had touched our lives. It was laughing about his eccentricities and remembering his triumphs. It brought him alive again in our hearts, even for just a moment.

No one said anything that upset my grief, but no one seemed to know and recognize the pain of losing a best friend. Society is filled with condolences for family members but less so for close friends. There's an old saying— friends are the family we'd choose for ourselves. Matt was my family and my home.

It was so hard to lose a best friend. And while I have deep, nurturing friendships with others now, no one has been as close or touched my heart as much as Matt. With his passing, I lost part of myself, and it will never return. I wish people would have recognized and honored the deep connection that close friends have and the deep pain that came with his passing.

> Treasure your friendships. Nurture them. Go deep with friends on the most important things and the most trivial things. The Greek philosopher Epicurus said, "Of all the means to ensure happiness throughout life, by far the most important is the acquisition of friends." I truly believe and practice this as much as I can. Friends go beyond family. They touch the soul in the most important and nourishing ways. Love and appreciate your friends while they're still here.
>
> When someone you know loses a friend, ask them about the friendship. Ask about what made them so close. Ask them to tell you the stories. Help them to heal by reliving and treasuring the memories that made them so special in their lives. God bless you, Matt Krapf; how I miss you, my dear friend.

After reading Mike's story about Matt, my only thought was, we should all be so lucky to have a friendship like theirs. When you know someone who's lost a friend, think of this beautiful story, and reach out to offer comfort and support.

Losing a close friend can feel like losing a big part of your life. You grieve the memories and the future without them. It can feel lonely if no one else understands how deep a loss it is. One way we can stay connected to our friends is through their families and/or other friends. Share memories, celebrate special dates, and keep in touch with each other. It helps a lot to be around others that also love them.

CHAPTER 16

LOSS TO SUICIDE

Suicide statistics in the US are alarming. According to the CDC, around 46,000 people died by suicide in 2020 in the U.S. that's one person every eleven minutes. The saddest statistic is that the third leading cause of death for children between ages ten and fourteen and the second leading cause of death for people between fifteen and thirty-four is suicide—the youth of our society.

I belong to two Facebook groups for parents who have lost a child to suicide, and every single day there are new photos representing new suicides. It's shocking to me how many are teens, some twelve years old or younger. I can't get used to it. Each time I read their names and see their beautiful, youthful faces, I wonder why. What made this child unable to continue living?

The most common reason for kids this age taking their own lives is bullying. If I could have one wish granted, it would be for everyone to treat each other with kindness. On the surface, it sounds naive, but imagine what the world would be like if we all looked out for each other, cared about one another, and treated each other with love and respect. It will never happen, but it's okay to be a dreamer sometimes.

A suicide death is unlike any other. When someone ends their life, their loved ones not only experience the heartbreak of the loss but go through an entire gamut of emotions. You may always wonder why the suicide happened. You'll feel less raw grief as time goes on. Eventually, you'll find comfort in honoring their memory.

Suicide may be the most uncomfortable type of death to experience and talk about. But please, don't let that stop you. A family grieving a loved one who took their own life has extra emotions and questions to deal with, so they need all the support they can get. Loved ones may worry about what others will think. There will be times when we wonder, "What could I have done differently?" The answer? Most likely nothing; someone who is determined will follow through no matter what.

Suicide terminology matters too. When we say, "She committed suicide," the connotation is negative. It makes the act of suicide sound like a crime or an offense. Instead, use a term like, "He took his life" or "She died by suicide."

When Keven died, my house was declared a "crime scene," and I wasn't allowed inside. I was forced to sit in the heat on a hot August day while the police and coroner spent hours processing the scene. It seemed unnecessary to me, almost cruel, to assume it was anything but a suicide. But they have guidelines to follow, and I had no choice. Being guarded by a police officer at my door was disturbing; the police didn't want me trying to sneak in (which I would have). I had to be escorted to the bathroom. What I really wanted was to see Keven again before they took him away, but they wouldn't allow it.

When they carried his body downstairs on a gurney, they

stopped and let our dog, Sugar, sniff him to let her know he was gone. I found it both odd and kind. Keven's body was in an opaque bag under a thick navy-blue blanket. I followed them all the way to the door of the coroner's van, and when they put him in the back, the blanket slid off his foot. I grabbed his foot through the bag and began wailing. I didn't want to let go. After a few seconds, they closed the doors, forcing me to drop his foot. I ran after the van for a few feet after it left my house, then dropped to my knees on the asphalt and sobbed uncontrollably.

Most people want to see their loved ones after they pass. I had already seen Keven and knew he looked good other than the hole above his right temple with the fountain of blood shooting out. I would see his body one more time on the day of the memorial service.

Some people judge the person who ended their life. I can see it in their eyes when they hear how my son died. Some even make remarks about him being selfish and not caring about me or my feelings. This hurts me and causes me to be very defensive. Depending on how well I know the person who makes a comment determines my reaction. If it's an acquaintance, I usually ignore it. If it's a friend, I go into my "lecture" about why Keven did it and how much I know we loved each other. I'm certain he waited until after his beloved grandma had passed because it may have broken her beyond repair. Kev knew I would be devastated but would survive and use his life to help others.

One thing suicide and a loss to drugs or alcohol have in common is the stigma attached to it. People can judge what they don't understand. If people continue to judge these types of deaths, it will be harder for people to ask for help. It causes shame instead of inviting support. There is no shame and no blame. Your loved one's choice will hurt you deeply, but it's nobody else's business to point out. If friends or family emphasize the "suicide" aspect and add their own ideas to further stigmatize it, don't let them add stress to your grief.

I believe in most cases, when a person takes their life, it's because the emotional pain and mental anguish they're suffering become unbearable, and they see no hope it will get better.

In December 2022, the entertainment community lost the beloved Stephen tWitch Boss. Many people know him as Ellen DeGeneres' DJ and dance partner on her talk show *Ellen* or the reality show *So You Think You Can Dance*. He was always smiling and dancing and had a beautiful family he loved. The day before he took his life, he posted a video of him and his wife doing a fun dance together.

Robin Williams, Anthony Bourdain, Naomi Judd, and Kate Spade are examples of well-known celebrities who have died by suicide in recent years (this is just to name a few). The seemingly cheerful people in your own life might be at risk, too. tWitch is the perfect example of putting on a smiling face for others. Sometimes pain looks like dance. When we lose a famous person to suicide, it's a reminder mental illness doesn't care how much success, money, or fame you have. It doesn't always show up in obvious ways. But it's there for many of us. It's tragic for those left behind, but for the person who ended their life, it's their perceived only chance at freedom from suffering.

Others may end their life spontaneously after an event like the end of a relationship. If they're suffering physical pain like terminal cancer, they may decide to take matters into their own hands. I have a friend whose mother chose assisted suicide because of an illness that left her unable to speak or care for herself. I think I might choose the same thing in that situation.

Another reason for suicide is to relieve someone of the "burden" of taking care of them. Sometimes someone does it to get out of financial debt or legal trouble. Recently, a high school principal in my area jumped to his death rather than face charges of child endangerment and battery. His court date was the following day.

The number one thing a person who's lost someone to suicide needs is empathy. Try not to let friends and family add stress to your grief by emphasizing the "suicide" aspect and adding their own ideas to further stigmatize it.

I chose not to seek professional help after Keven died. He'd warned me for years, and I'd imagined it a thousand times, so although it was a shock, it was not surprising. Therapists can be a big help and provide healthy coping strategies to begin healing and acceptance. So can support groups for suicide loss, as well as close friends and families who listen without adding their opinions.

HERE ARE SOME COMMON MISUNDERSTANDINGS ABOUT SUICIDE:

Myth # 1 It's dangerous to ask a depressed person whether they've considering suicide. You may be hesitant to bring up suicide with a vulnerable person because the fear of mentioning it might prompt them to follow through. Feeling heard allows people to think out loud and process what they're going through. You can suggest they seek help once they feel heard. Whenever you suspect someone you love is considering suicide, reach out to them. Reminding them they're cared for and valued may give them the strength to ask for help. Also, if the worst happens and they follow through, you will know without a doubt you were there for them. After Keven's death, I heard from a lot of his friends who said, "I should have done more; maybe I could have stopped him." I assured them he knew they loved him, they didn't have to feel this way, and he was determined; no one could stop him.

Myth # 2 People take their own life "out of the blue." Almost everyone who takes their own life has been thinking about it for a long time. More times than not, there are warning signs, including telling others they want to end their lives, giving away possessions, acting recklessly, having dramatic mood swings, abusing substances, and withdrawing from family and friends. Bearing witness to this can be upsetting, but it's your chance to offer support before it's too late. I saw the signs with Doug and wondered if I lived closer, would I have been able to stop him? I felt bad for months and finally had to let it go.

Myth # 3 Someone who has a great life isn't at risk. No matter how great someone's life looks from the outside, even those we think "have it all" can be at risk. Unless they tell us or show us through actions, we don't know what they're feeling. When you see someone exhibit warning signs for suicide, don't brush it off. Reach out to them. Have an honest conversation. One conversation isn't enough. Keep in touch and let them know they are not alone.

Myth # 4 Most suicides happen around the winter holiday season. I've always heard this, but when I researched it, I learned the highest rate is in the springtime. According to Dr. Adam Kaplin, Johns Hopkins assistant professor of psychiatry and behavioral sciences, "April, May, and June, the suicide rate goes up and is the highest." Those numbers can be two to three times higher than in December, when suicide rates are the lowest.

Myth # 5 When someone seems to have made progress in their depression, their risk of suicide lessens. Unfortunately, this myth can be a sign they've made their decision and feel "excited" that the end is near. It takes planning and preparation to perform the act of suicide. Sometimes feeling better provides the jolt of energy it takes to get it done. So, it's important not to assume someone is better. Please keep checking on them, talking to them, and making sure they know they are not alone and there's hope.

Myth # 6 Giving someone a hotline number to call is enough. Thousands of people call every year for help with suicidal thoughts. Suicide hotlines can be effective but are just one part of the big picture. I'm thrilled they finally created a short three-digit number to call, 988, for the suicide prevention hotline, but I think personal contact and face-to-face conversations help much more. You never know who will be on the other end of the phone. A friend told me they made him feel worse, not better.

Myth # 7 A stay at a "mental hospital" will fix them.
If someone threatens suicide, they can be taken to the nearest hospital and will be put on a 72-hour hold. Not all hospitals have a behavioral health unit, so if the situation isn't urgent, call and ask. I learned this the first time Keven attempted suicide. He was 18. He was brought to our local hospital via ambulance but was later transferred. If someone has a failed attempt, even if they argue against it, do all you can to get them help. During this time, they will be observed, kept safe, and diagnosed. Seventy-two hours is not long enough to do

much good. But it's a start. My county has C.A.T. - Centralized Assessment Team. If you call, they will send out a team to evaluate someone in their home and provide help. Sometimes, they may bring the person to the hospital without their consent (for example, if they are in psychosis). They always bring a police officer along, which is understandable, but that's the reason I never called them. Keven would freak out every time the police came near our house.

Myth # 8 Suicide is selfish or cowardly.
I take this one personally. The most common thing people say after a suicide death is "how selfish" it was. There's an overwhelming belief this is true, and sometimes, it may be. Even some professionals think this. When the coroner and her assistant were at my home after Keven's death, the assistant looked me in the eye and said, "Suicide is selfish." I was in shocked numbness. It had only been hours since Keven died, so that's my excuse for not punching the guy in the nose. Seriously, I would not have punched him, but I would have given him a lecture on what *not to* say to a person who just lost someone to suicide. Suicide is *not* selfish.

Most people hold off if they can before taking their life. Despite trying for years, hopelessness and depression wears them down to the point where they feel they had no choice but to give up. While knowing they'll hurt their loved ones may keep them around longer, if nothing changes mentally or emotionally, relief becomes more important than hurting people.

In addition to calling suicide selfish, some people say only cowards do it. I'm sure you've guessed my thoughts on this. This is a poem Keven wrote after one of his failed attempts.

How Far Can You Get
They say suicide is for cowards
But let's see how far you get
Holding your head to a railroad track trying to
forget
Or the barrel in your mouth, finger itching on the
trigger
Let's see how many pills you take before you can't
remember
Let's see how long you take to jump with a noose
around your neck
But seriously, let's see how far you get.

— KEVEN LEGERE

The person who ends their life by suicide sees it as the only solution. They've tried everything they know of to get beyond the hopelessness, but nothing (not even drugs) could lift them out of the pit.

On May 1, 2019, Harv Jamison lost his son, Brian, the same way I lost Keven, a self-inflicted gunshot wound to the right temple. Brian was also the same age, 29 years old. I asked him to share his story.

THOUGHTS FROM A FATHER ON SUICIDE LOSS—HARV JAMISON:

> I think about Brian every waking hour and feel sadness for the good life mental illness robbed him of. After his death, I didn't process his loss very well. I couldn't close my eyes at night without seeing him in my garage after he pulled the

trigger— his brain destroyed by the .22 round. I fell victim to drinking to numb the pain. It didn't take long for me to become a full-fledged alcoholic and fall into a deep depression. After nearly a year and a half of drunk crying, my ex-wife Cheryl admitted me to Synergy Executive, which offered a 30-day inpatient rehab with classes, therapy, and world-class accommodations.

Cheryl insisted I stay with her after rehab so she could protect me from temptations. But EMDR therapy in rehab allowed me to process grief in a healthy manner. Today, I've been sober for over two years. After nine years of divorce, we got along so well we decided to make the situation permanent and sold our homes and bought a new home to share our "golden years".

Keeping busy is my best therapy nowadays. I retired at age sixty-three after Brian's first suicide attempt and moved him in to live with me. After he was gone, it seemed my life no longer had purpose, and I felt like a failure in being unable to save him. I was offered a part-time job as a legal videographer a couple of years ago, a job I find fascinating and am grateful to have. Social media has been a wonderful outlet for me to post videos about my experiences in dealing with grief, loss, and sobriety. I've connected with many others who have also had a difficult time processing grief.

Brian was diagnosed with schizophrenia after being hospitalized following his first suicide attempt.

Brian didn't want to die. Mental illness struck him when he was in his mid-20s and literally destroyed any semblance of normalcy. His mind was preoccupied with paranoid thoughts—the government was "out to get him," he was under federal indictment, his family would be imprisoned if he didn't sacrifice himself. I have a video I took with my phone of him sitting outside his bedroom, crying and begging God to save him.

Severe mental illness isn't easily treated. The medical community seems to treat patients mainly by prescribing a wide variety of meds, which may or may not be effective. For those afflicted by depression, bipolar, borderline personality, and especially schizophrenia, getting proper help is a challenge.

Brian had good days and bad. The last few days before the end, he was very withdrawn and scared. May 1st, 2019, began as a good day—perfect weather and clear blue skies. Brian was even in a good mood. Around noon, he wanted to go out for lunch. He wanted to go to Wendy's, but I insisted we have some Chinese food (since I was buying). In retrospect, I regret the decision. After we returned home, he said he had a project to complete in the garage. Nothing unusual about that—he occupied his time with building custom speakers and playing with music production software on an elaborate computer system.

I went in and stretched out on my bed and scrolled around on my iPad. I must have dozed off. I awoke suddenly, got up, and went through the kitchen to go out to the garage. When I heard the noise, I paused. I soon found out it was called agonal breathing. I opened the door and saw Brian's prone body twitching and the horrible sound of moaning. Red flowed under his head as I walked over. It took a moment to realize it was blood. His eyes were almost closed. I saw the small handgun in his right hand and plucked it out of this grip and placed it on a workbench. I quickly called 911 and told them my son had shot himself in the head.

A female police officer arrived within a minute. Then another, then two more squad cars. Then an ambulance and

> a fire truck. An EMT began chest compressions while a gurney was wheeled in to transport him to the hospital.
>
> I called Cheryl. By the time we got to the ER, Brian was on life support. We were escorted to the room where he was hooked up to wires and tubes. The doctor solemnly told us Brian had no brain activity—the damage was too severe. I insisted they do more testing, which they did. Same thing. We finally give them permission to turn off the machines.
>
> We spent a little time with Brian. He was cleaned up, although the head bandage hadn't quite stopped the trickle of blood dribbling down into his ear.
>
> Gorman-Scharpf Funeral Home did an excellent job of making him presentable for us, and we spent 45 minutes with him. We had already planned for cremation, but he looked so good I almost decided on an open casket. We all cried and said our goodbyes. And that was it – twenty-nine years of caring for and loving this beautiful young man since infancy. Gone way too soon, but always alive in our hearts.

I've released the trauma of seeing Kev in the aftermath of his death (see Resources in the back of the book for an excellent recommendation on releasing trauma). On a day-to-day basis, I feel whatever comes up. I don't fight it or hold it in because letting it out helps me move forward in a healthy way.

To show how sad a suicidal person can be, Kev wrote these short poems:

Looking for Solace
I run through the darkest recesses of my mind,
Looking for something I cannot find
Something, I don't know what it is,

But I know it's my escape from this ugly haunted
place
My mind races as I look, but all I see are empty
pages of a book
The place I am at is completely black
And makes pleasant thoughts turn to ash
So, I turn back and look again
But there's nothing but oblivion

— KEVEN LEGERE

Zero

I am nothing to this world
Just an empty hole immersed
The books I read
The shows I watched
My soul, they cannot touch
The windows are glazed
From where I stand
To everyone I cry in despair
I am nothing
I am zero

— KEVEN LEGERE

Each time my heart breaks,
It becomes harder to heal
And hope fades
Into desolation
Loneliness and despair
Which turns to self-hatred and self-loathing
But soon it will be over
But soon it will end

Because I found you my only friend
Bang, bang, now I'm dead.

— KEVEN LEGERE

Please treat the family and friends who've lost someone to suicide as you would any other grieving person. People who have lost a loved one in this way are hurting and heartbroken. Remember, they may carry an extra burden of guilt, shame, or defensiveness. Some consider this type of death the most difficult of all. Nobody should have to grieve alone, even after a death by suicide. I hope society will stop looking at suicide as a sin, or a weakness, drop the judgment, and gain some compassion.

For those who know this devastating loss, don't forget your loved one wasn't leaving you. They were leaving a life they couldn't handle. It has nothing to do with their love for you.

CHAPTER 17
LOSS TO MURDER

Another traumatic type of death we don't talk about a lot is death by murder. Losing someone to murder is unimaginable to me. The anger at knowing someone purposely and brutally took my loved one away would eat away at my heart and soul. Stephanie Swanson, a mom who works as an ER Nurse and has an incredible presence on TikTok sharing her wisdom and experience on grief with other parents, shares her story here.

THOUGHTS FROM A MOTHER ON MURDER—STEPHANIE SWANSON:

> My son, Joshuah, was surrounded in an apartment and shot to death by six police officers on January 18, 2018. He was thirty-six years old. While in a mental health crisis, he took two handguns and a safe from my house. Police reports vary on what really took place that morning. It has become one of the many unanswerable questions we have to live with.

Joshuah sustained a closed head injury when he was twenty-three and was never the same after. As his depression spiraled, he got into self-medicating by using street drugs, including heroin, Methamphetamine, Xanax, and Ecstasy. His perception of reality changed to paranoia and obsessive thoughts requiring psychiatric hospitalization for over a year.

When he was released, he was no longer an addict, but the psych medications made him shake, rock, and drool, making living alone impossible. He slowly weaned himself off the psych meds, but he still battled what we called "cycling." He would be normal for weeks at a time, but then obsessions and paranoia would take over. Usually, it lasted a few days.

Joshuah was always "on," meaning his hyper-awareness and ability to turn everything into laughter could overwhelm even the most patient person. He primarily lived with his older sister, but we shared in caring for him. It was a lot to handle him.

Joshuah's sisters grieved in their own ways, his death being their first major loss of someone they deeply loved. Their motto was, "We are a tripod, from the womb to the tomb."

Our family get-togethers have a glaring void we acknowledge. There is a collective sadness that permeates every celebration. We talk about him. Our memories and the situations Joshuah created often bring us back to laughter, just as he intended. And for a moment, he's present in our collective laughter. Then, we all get quiet and sigh as the heaviness of our loss settles back into the room. This is how we grieve together.

I wish people knew I don't mind talking about my son or what happened to him. The pain of his irrelevance to those

> who ended his life adds to the overall despair. No parent wants their child's life to be pointless and forgotten. I want his life to be bigger than his death, and the only way to achieve this is to talk about him, about how funny he was, how he loved homeless people, how he sacrificed gas money to buy a disheveled and unloved man cigarettes. This is who he was and how his family will remember him.

Very few people experience what it's like to lose someone to a violent act that ends in death. If you know someone who's experienced this type of loss, they might be feeling very isolated. There is anger that goes hand in hand with this type of grief as well as horrific thoughts about how it happened. Please be extra kind and supportive to someone grieving this tragic loss. Let them know you want to be there to listen to whatever they are feeling.

CHAPTER 18
LOSS TO DRUGS & ALCOHOL

Drug overdoses are also traumatic deaths that have a stigma attached and therefore leave the griever feeling lonely and/or shamed. According to the National Center for Drug Abuse Statistics, 96,779 deaths occurred between March 2020 and March 2021 alone. With today's fentanyl crisis, these numbers are climbing.

Imagine each of those people leaving behind parents, siblings, grandparents, cousins, aunts, uncles, friends, co-workers, and neighbors. Millions are grieving this type of loss. If you are one of them, you may feel alone. Finding others who could relate helped me so much after I lost Anthony.

Substance abuse and addiction are still misunderstood and judged a lot. Substance use disorders often go hand in hand with mental health issues. This stigma applies to anyone who suffers from mental illness as well. Like suicide loss, people are quick to blame the victim and judge the family.

With drugs, the old stereotype still exists: "Drug addicts are bad people who live in the streets and don't care about anyone but themselves." Things are slowly changing. By now, our society should know that people of all classes, races, religions, political affiliations, and sexual orientations struggle with substance use disorder (drugs or alcohol). It's a disease.

In their "Public Policy Statement: Definition of Addiction," written in August 2011, the American Society of Addiction Medicine says this:

> Addiction is a primary, chronic disease of brain reward, motivation, memory, and related circuitry. Consistent differences in neurophysiology between addicts and non-addicts have been observed. Addicts are more impulsive and have difficulties with judgment and decision-making. They have memory problems that make it difficult to plan a schedule or get things done, and they have difficulty describing how they feel or recognizing how other people feel.

People don't choose addiction or alcoholism. Many of them lose everything and still struggle for years to find sobriety.

There's a lot less empathy for addicts and alcoholics because it's assumed they're aware of the risks and don't deserve sympathy. I shared this story in *Keven's Choice,* but it's a perfect example of what I'm talking about:

> In 2010 my friend, Maggie, lost her firstborn of four sons, Mitchell, to an accidental overdose. She attended several grief support groups for parents and soon discovered that her loss was treated with less compassion and empathy than others—as if her pain over the loss of Mitch wasn't as valid as a parent who lost a child to cancer or an accident. She decided that there was a need for a specific group for those who had lost their children to drugs.
>
> Maggie took it upon herself to start the group, and it's called Solace for Hope. It's a non-profit organization with

> both in-person (Southern California only so far) and online meetings, plus a Facebook group. Solace offers a safe and compassionate place for family members and friends who have been impacted by Substance Use Disorder and loss. It's become like a family to me and many others I've met there.

The most serious problem with this type of stigma is that it makes it hard for people that need help to ask for it. Every time I think we're making progress in breaking the stigma against substance use disorder, I come across nasty things people continue to say or believe. People continue to argue addiction/substance use disorder isn't a disease; it's a choice, even though it's scientifically proven to be one.

It's my hope that someday people who have the disease of substance use disorder—whether they use alcohol, opiates, or any other substance—are treated with the same respect people with diabetes, cancer, or other diseases are. We all start out the same: innocent and dependent on those around us to survive. In between birth and death, we are each born into different circumstances and face unique challenges in our lives. Some of us can drink alcohol casually and stop when we want; some of us can't. Some try drugs and carry on with life. Others try drugs and discover they can numb their pain, then find themselves in a pit of self-destruction.

Most people I know who have this disease are creative, sensitive, intelligent people (and I've met hundreds over my lifetime). They are typically harder on themselves than we are. There's a good chance they feel hopeless, alone, unworthy, and guilty. They love others but can't love themselves. They feel remorse knowing they cause their loved ones worry, stress, and other issues.

Gabor Mate is a highly regarded expert in mental health, trauma, and addiction. Here is how he sees addiction:

> What if we replaced the word 'addict' with: 'A human being who suffered so much he or she finds in drugs or some other behavior a temporary escape from suffering'?

The last thing the family member of an addict deserves is judgment. We are suffering enough without hearing whispers about our parenting. But ignorance lives on. There are still people who think they can prevent their child from ever trying a drug, convinced they "raised them right." The three most dangerous words a parent can say is, "Not my kid."

There's one last thing I'd like to bring up regarding drug overdose deaths. At the risk of angering a whole segment of parents who've lost a child to fentanyl, I have a humble request. When you lose someone because they unknowingly took a pill or substance laced with a lethal dose of fentanyl, you label it as murder or, more commonly, poisoning. I understand. But in addition, some parents say with indignation, "My child was *not* an addict!" This is painful for someone who lost a loved one to substance use disorder. They usually struggle for years, trying to find recovery. They are not "less than" because they have substance use disorder. I hope you can refrain from using that term. If you insist on clarifying your child was not an addict, it causes more stigma against addicts and more heartache to their loved ones.

What do parents of addicts hear when a parent loses their child to something laced with fentanyl? "My child wasn't an addict," I can answer after many tearful and angry conversations with families impacted by this statement. We hear and feel:

- My loved one deserved to die, but yours didn't.
- My loved one asked for what they got, but your child is an innocent victim of murder by poisoning.

- Addicts are losers, unworthy of the empathy people who die from fentanyl deserve.
- You raised your kids right, and I didn't.
- My loved one chose death by taking the risk; yours didn't know any better.
- Laws should be changed because "good people" are dying even though hundreds of thousands of our loved ones have died from heroin and opiate pills for decades, and no one seems to care.

Maybe we could change the narrative. Maybe when people say, "My child was not an addict," the phrase can evoke these thoughts:

- I didn't suffer in fear or endure the unbearable things a parent of an addict had to experience.
- My grief didn't start years before my child died like parents of addicted children did.
- My child didn't endure the horrific lifestyle many addicts have, so they didn't know what it felt like to be looked down upon, lose everything, and fight for their life.
- Although we lost our children to drugs in different ways, their child and their loss are as significant and painful as mine; in fact, it's probably more so.

Ten years ago, my friend, Maggie Fleitman, started a grief support group for parents who lost their children to overdose (it's grown to include suicide). She recognized the need after being shunned by parents in a support group who lost children to illness and accidents. Can you imagine? As if their son's death from accidental overdose wasn't important and didn't deserve the same empathy.

Losing someone to drugs or alcohol feels like a double loss for those who have been watching their loved one struggle for years. Please keep this in mind when you meet someone who's experienced this type of loss. Give them more compassion, not less.

If you're interested in hearing about what it's like to be an addict and a parent of an addict, check out my book *Keven's Choice*.

HOPE FOR THE GRIEVER

Sadly, we are not alone. There are many other people grieving similar losses, and when we find each other, we have found the only other people who truly get what we're going through. This kind of empathy is invaluable as we move through our grief. Look for a support group online or in person. It's the number one thing that's helped me.

CHAPTER 19

GRIEVING THE LIVING

Sometimes we grieve for a person who's still here with us. They could have a terminal illness that drags on as you watch them slowly come to the end of their life. There could be a debilitating disease that makes them frail and incapable of taking care of themselves. It could be Alzheimer's, MS, ALS, or a mental illness that changes them. Or they could have substance use disorder.

My friend Bob Edwards knows exactly what it's like to grieve someone who's still here, on top of losing his first wife, Ellen. So I asked him to share about his precious wife, Ann, and the challenges they faced. He is among the kindest, most generous, caring people I know. It's painful for me to see what he and Ann endure each day.

THOUGHTS FROM A SPOUSE ON HIS WIFE'S ILLNESS—BOB EDWARDS:

After my first wife, Ellen, died, I was not sure I would ever find a woman I could love as much. Meeting Ann was a total surprise. We had known each other since the 70s but never had a conversation more than the occasional 'hi' as we passed in the hallway at work. Finding Ann was like an answer to a prayer I had never prayed—although I prayed a lot back then.

After we married in 1995, Ann moved in with me and my kids. She was solid and was a blessing to our family. She loved my children, and after years, they began to connect with her. Life was certainly different for the kids—they were still grieving the loss of their mom. I could tell, for them, opening their hearts to Ann meant closing a bit of their hearts to their mother's memory. Grief is such a messy phenomenon.

Life sailed by. Our daughter got pregnant in high school—it was difficult to experience the alienation happening as she moved out in her last semester to live with her boyfriend. While this was happening, my son had also moved out and I worried about his drug issues. My life seemed to be falling apart.

During the chaos, Ann had surgery to remove a large benign tumor from her uterus. The surgery was successful. I remember the morning I picked her up. Ann began to slur her words as I walked into her room and could not stand; I thought she was having a stroke. Days later, the doctors ruled out a stroke and thought she might have Multiple Sclerosis (MS). Yet they could not say for sure.

I watched Ann learn to walk again. The whole experience

was traumatizing. Yet there seemed to be an end to it as Ann recovered and our lives returned to almost normal. Meanwhile, our daughter delivered the baby and graduated from high school in May. A few months later, Ann had another relapse (of what they thought to be MS) but without the disabling effects. She went on the first of many MS drugs, and things again returned to the new-not-normal.

After a hellish year, we decided to go on a Caribbean cruise. I remember the anticipation of being on vacation over the holidays. Within a day of departure, Ann began experiencing the symptoms of a relapse of her disease. Watching her decline overnight was the most traumatic thing I had been through to date, more so than watching my first wife die.

As Ann lay in our stateroom, paralyzed from the waist down, I went up on the deck as she napped. I remember stepping into the hot tub and hearing a still, small voice within. The voice spoke to me of not trying to manage the situation but to flow with it. This message of 'flowing' and not 'managing' became my life's new mantra.

Life went on, and Ann recovered, but not quite to the level she was at before. Again we were experiencing a new normal. Unfortunately, Ann would have several more relapses in the following years. The doctors had a hard time treating her and preventing the relapses. As her caregiver, it was so hard to watch and experience with her.

In the summer of 2007, Ann experienced a mega-relapse that left her unable to walk and needing a wheelchair to get around. The doctors had no clue about the origins of the relapse but deemed it to be a progression of MS as they looked at MRI images that revealed new damages to her nervous system.

Ann came home in a wheelchair. We bought a ramped-accessible van and took our first trip to Ann's father's funeral in January 2008. It was a crazy and traumatic time. This new normal was killing us. Then, a few months later, things changed for us again. Ann had another surgery and another major relapse. She was re-diagnosed with an autoimmune disease called Neuromyelitis Optica (NMO).

It is hard to put into words how upset, angry, and traumatized I was. Over the years, I challenged the MS diagnosis but was not 'heard' when I voiced my concerns. Dealing with a disabling disease is often unbearable and just plain frustrating.

Yet all along, I tried to remember the words I heard as I stepped into the hot tub so many years ago. I began dealing with my controlling nature and tried to flow more as life took turns for the worse. Over the years, I have been to different counselors, but they seemed overwhelmed by what I told them. I think grieving losses like disability is different than grieving losses like death or divorce.

In June of 2010, Ann and I moved to a loft in the river area of downtown Kansas City. The move gave Ann a lot of freedom as she could get her hair cut, shop for groceries, go to the dentist, and do many other things she couldn't do in the suburbs.

A year later, Ann had a new experimental stem cell procedure done at a hospital in downtown Chicago. She had chemo treatments before to prepare her and lost her hair. The stem cell transplant went without a hitch. Then, just a few days later, Ann caught a bug and had no immune system to fight it off. Ann went on a respirator for seven days. Her sister flew in from Kansas, and we were unsure if she would make it.

Caring for a disabled person is always hard. Even the

most minor things can disrupt our lives. Yet sitting at Ann's bedside in the hospital seemed to bring me to a new level of trauma and anxiety. The day they removed the feeding tube was so joyful. Yet a month of inpatient therapy was needed to prepare Ann to cope at home in Kansas City.

Being away from home for the summer was difficult. Coming home was both joyous and challenging. Being a caregiver for a person in a wheelchair is never a dull life. Everything takes longer. Patience is on trial every day. Friendships are difficult to forge. Yet life goes on.

I have two friends helping me cope with life. I speak with them weekly, and we often share a meal, coffee, or a few beers. They have been a lifeline at times. People who 'just listen' can have such a healing influence. It is hard to cry at times, but the empathy of these two friends encourages me when nothing else does.

In early 2020 Ann was having a difficult time getting out of bed. I took hold of her, as I had at other times, and she just collapsed. I heard something in my back snap, and we both found ourselves on the floor. I called 911, and before I knew it, Ann was in the hospital again. Months later, Ann would come home to another new normal.

The doctors did not know why Ann lost her ability to stand. They told me it was just a progression of her disease, but they were unable to speak to any specificity. I scrambled to deal with her new level of disability and installed two (expensive) overhead lift systems in our loft.

Dealing with ramps, walkers, wheelchairs, broken elevators, accessible vans, standing poles, and other devices have been a part of my life for twenty years. Yet dealing with permanent and portable lifts has taken Ann's dependency on me to a new level. I use the lifts to transfer Ann to and from her wheelchair in the bedroom and the bathroom. This increased caregiving demand has put a lot of stress on me in my post-seventy years.

Dealing with the stress of caregiving is overwhelming. Being responsible for another person when I am having my health issues wipes me out. Much of the time, I do not know what to do. I am stressed and traumatized so much as I watch Ann struggle.

Small things push me over the edge and greatly stress me out. We find ourselves talking about what life looks like in the year ahead, and, honestly, the future looks dark. We live like shut-ins.

Along with the grief I experience, there's an awareness that there's someone whose grief eclipses mine, Ann. Each day I see Ann grieving the loss of her legs and other parts of her body. Ann deals with neurological pain and failures of organs in her body. The grace with which she copes profoundly amazes me.

I am not sure I have learned a lot these past twenty years, but I think it is important for me to let go of my life and try not to control things that are not meant to be controlled. It is not easy, but I think it is necessary.

You don't have to lose someone to death to grieve them. When you lose the person they once were, there's a different type of pain and sadness because you watch them suffer. With death, suffering is over, and we're grieving for ourselves for missing them. This type of grief is just as painful, and sometimes more so.

HOPE FOR THE GRIEVER

Feeling helpless is a part of this type of grief. However, we need to remember even though it feels like there's nothing we can do, just being there for them is a powerful way to support them in their suffering. There are some resources in the back of the book that may be helpful.

CHAPTER 20

LIVING WITH A CHRONIC ILLNESS

Lee Varon has experienced many challenges over her lifetime, her story inspires me because of her resilience and positive outlook. She's experienced the loss of a healthy body to a challenging disease that has a significant impact on her quality of life.

Lee has authored a book that I highly recommend *My Brother Is Not a Monster: A Story of Addiction and Recovery.* It's written as a children's book but is an excellent resource for parents, teachers, or any adult working to support a young person with a family member dealing with substance use disorder.

LIVING WITH A CHRONIC ILLNESS—LEE VARON:

I sat in the tall examining chair, clutching the padded armrests.

"You mean you can't see anything," the bespeckled

optometrist said as he peered down at me. "Not even the big E at the top?"

"No, nothing," I said. And then, in a shaky voice, "Is it serious?"

"It could be," he responded, advising me to go immediately to Mass Eye and Ear.

I trudged through the wet snow to see the optometrist. Now I sat in his office, looking (or trying to look) at the eye chart lit up on the opposite wall. The vision in my right eye was the same, but when he covered that eye and asked me to read the chart, I desperately searched for anything to grasp onto.

It was 1981. The MRI had just been invented but was yet to be in use, even in major hospitals. My blindness was ruled an isolated incident of optic neuritis. Cause unknown. The word MS was mentioned once by one of the young interns at Mass Eye and Ear, but I quickly put that out of my mind and clung to the words: *isolated incident.* I never regained full vision in that eye. I was left with shadows and forms and not enough vision to distinguish color, read, drive, or even walk easily. Fortunately, I still had my right eye.

Please, God, I prayed, *don't let me lose anything else.* I was working as a counselor at a women's health collective, but I suddenly felt as overwhelmed by life as many of the women I was supposed to counsel. Having lost sight, I often felt ill-equipped to help others.

Over the next decade, I was visited by a host of symptoms: severe fatigue that seemed to rise out of nowhere, leaving me as limp as a wrung-out dishrag, brain fog that left me feeling disoriented, bouts of dizziness and sometimes even vertigo which made it impossible to carry out daily tasks, aching muscles, and, most frighteningly for me, blurriness in my good eye. I can still remember one afternoon sitting across from a woman I was counseling, only to have her face blur into the rose-colored wallpaper behind her. A constant hum of anxiety accompanied all of these symptoms.

MS has been called *the disease of a thousand faces,* and it seems to affect people in wildly different ways. I had a friend who died of the disease at forty-five, and another who's nearly eighty and still travels all over the world.

It was nearly a decade after my attack of optic neuritis before I had another major exacerbation. In my early 40s, I woke up and couldn't move my legs. They were there but felt numb and tingly, and my feet felt like ice blocks. I was taken to the doctor, who promptly ordered an MRI—the clanging and knocking tunnel I would become familiar with. The MRI showed my brain and spinal cord covered with lesions—little white smudges the doctor showed me on my MRI film.

"You've had MS for ten years," the doctor explained.

I sat on the cold examining table in a paper gown as the doctor—one of the best neurologists in Boston—examined me. She was young and perky, and as I sat trembling, she patted my arm: "Oh there, there now, don't be so nervous," she said, smiling.

Fine for her to say; she hadn't just been told her whole life was changing forever! Though never an athlete, I loved hiking, camping, and bike riding. In my twenties, I'd traveled all over Europe on a Eurail pass. Now I felt my entire life crumbling away.

Some people with chronic illnesses speak of a loss of self. Newly diagnosed, I wondered how much of my old self I would lose.

Initially, I alternated between denying my diagnosis would affect me at all and embracing my new identity as a person with a disability. Soon after my diagnosis, I went to a weekend retreat for people who recently learned they had MS. I had regained most of the function of my legs, but they would never be the same. So I thought I'd tackle this beast head-on. But after watching young athletes playing wheelchair basketball and a woman who struggled to transition from her wheelchair to the toilet, I jumped into denial. It's hard, though, to live totally in denial when your body keeps reminding you that you're not "normal." Eventually, I settled into some middle zone—I accepted that MS wasn't going away but tried not to dwell on it daily. Instead, I educated myself about the disease. However, living with chronic illness meant living with what-ifs; *What if I wake up and can't walk? What if I lose sight in my good eye?*

I've lived with MS now for over four decades. I've lived more years with MS than without it. As my peers age, they are starting to experience some of the symptoms I have experienced for decades. There are periods I walk with a cane and periods I need to take time off to recharge my batteries. MS has made me more compassionate with myself and with others. I've strengthened my faith in a God who, I feel, accompanies me throughout my life. When new or weird symptoms arise, I pray they will pass and do whatever I can to deal with them.

Many people with chronic illnesses know what it's like to lose things. But losing functions of the body doesn't mean you are losing yourself. On the contrary, MS has strengthened me in unexpected ways. I hope I've gained more patience, gratitude, compassion, and above all, persistence.

CHAPTER 21

LOSS OF A FUTURE

Grieving for the future can happen after an injury or illness has forced you to change your life plans. It can happen in several ways; here are a few:

- After a breakup with someone you thought you'd be with forever.
- When you find out none of your children are going to make you a grandparent.
- You're diagnosed with a terminal illness.
- You make a mistake that costs you your job or your life savings.

I asked my friend Donna to share her experience of grieving the future she felt was her calling in life.

THOUGHTS FROM SOMEONE WHO LOST HER CAREER —DONNA VANHORN:

It was unexpected. I was in my 40s and entering a career path; I hadn't dreamed about professional ministry. I also hadn't dreamed of going to school again, much less seminary, yet there I was, a former college dropout with a little more than a year left to complete a master's degree.

It was an exciting time. I was ordained and co-pastoring a small punk rock church in Portland, Oregon. I loved everything about it, especially the people.

Then a simple phone call brought the most unexpected news: the "C" word. Cancer had invaded my body.

To say life changed at that moment is an understatement. I was diagnosed with two kinds of invasive breast cancer, which looked to have metastasized in my ovaries. After that, everything was moving at a fast pace. Seminary was put on hold, and they rushed me into surgery. Three surgeries in one day: a hysterectomy with a bilateral oophorectomy, a bilateral mastectomy, and the start of reconstruction. The bright spot was when the test results returned negative for cancer in my ovaries. It's the one time I was glad my doctors were wrong.

Through this, my church community provided fierce support. They and folks from the seminary made our life bearable; they made me love them even more than I already did.

This was my first surgery, and I quickly learned that "recovery" is a serious word involving a lot of work. Nevertheless, my excitement to finish seminary and get on with my church work did not wane. If anything, it became the driving force to recover as quickly as possible.

The one thing about cancer is even once you get the all-clear from surgery, you still live with the possibility of a bomb going off in your body at any given time. Feeling like there was no time to waste, I dove back into seminary almost immediately. My co-pastors graciously worked around my schedule, and after the first term at school, I had to admit I couldn't do it all. It was difficult, but I took a leave of absence from my pastoral duties to focus on healing and school.

Little did I know taking a leave of absence would become the beginning of the end for me at the church. I tried to stay engaged by attending services and opening and closing when my co-pastors needed help. One of my final classes was an independent study about nature and spirituality. The professor allowed me to create a small group with the church to read and discuss what I was learning. It was a much-needed lifeline to stay involved. I was counting the days until graduation, so I could return to work and focus my energy on the community I loved.

Then the unexpected happened again; it was even more blindsiding than my cancer diagnosis; at least then, I felt bad and knew something was wrong.

I was completely caught off guard when the direction of a check-in meeting with my co-pastors changed. They questioned my desire to be a pastor; it was a punch to the gut that left me dazed and confused.

Some decisions are easier than others to make. Resigning from my job at the church was excruciatingly painful. I knew I didn't have the energy to fight, and while encouraged by others to start a new church, I knew I didn't have the energy for that either. I mostly didn't want to split our community, so I walked away. It wasn't what I wanted to do, but I didn't feel I had a choice. It was never explained to the congregation, and as leaders of a community that espoused vulnerability, we were anything but.

Cancer was a pain to deal with, but one I didn't question. Losing the community I loved is something I continue to grieve a decade later. I finished seminary, but it wasn't easy emotionally and physically. There was little joy in the accomplishment of graduating; considering my past, it was a huge deal, yet it became overshadowed by the loss of my job. The "path" I had been on was gone, obliterated by cancer treatments, recovery, and the weight of other people's expectations.

I know I'm lucky to be alive and grateful for that. It's still sad to think about what could have been if cancer had not invaded my body. So many what-ifs. It's not a grief I understood before. It's taught me love carries with it the ability to wound; it doesn't matter if what we love is a person, a pet, or a community.

Grieving isn't always about death; losing a career or any future plan, can be devastating. Making big plans or working towards goals that are shot down is a disappointing and life-changing loss.

HOPE FOR THE GRIEVER

Time will show you if there is a better plan for you in place. Accepting the loss after grieving it may bring new plans or ideas to your life. You may someday look back and see how this loss triggered your whole new way of life.

CHAPTER 22
LOSS OF A PET

Losing a beloved pet carries its own unique grief. For many of us, our pets are part of our families, or "our babies". Our pets are innocent creatures who love us unconditionally, provide us with support, entertainment, and sometimes are the reason we get up in the morning. My two dogs, Chester B, and Evo, are an essential part of my grief process. They give me someone to love, pamper, and snuggle with. Of course, they don't replace Keven, but they receive some of the love and affection I have stored up inside; I can't imagine not having them in my life.

Pet loss is hard to understand if you've never had one. Most people are compassionate toward the griever who is sharing about their pet loss, but I've heard comments such as, "It was just a dog", completely dismissing the person's loss.

Animals are capable of love, and sometimes they die after losing an owner. This happened in our family. My mother had a stroke that sent her to the hospital, put her in a coma, and ended her life. Her faithful dog, Chloe, anxiously waited for her to return home. We gave Chloe lots of love and attention and tried to explain that her "mom" wasn't coming home. She died quietly ten days after my mom.

When I first met Heidi Le, I instantly bonded with her over our love of pets. She shares her stories of losing a beloved cat and dog.

ON THE LOSS OF A PET—HEIDI LEE:

Two years ago, our cat, Smushy, passed away suddenly at a young age. We believe he choked to death on a hairball in the middle of the night. I had just given him his hairball medicine before bed, and when I found him in the morning, he was gone. It was so horrific and heartbreaking. I tearfully shared the news with a few friends and family members, mostly asking for prayer to help me get through what was already going to be a difficult day—our last day to move everything out of our house before turning the keys over to the new owners. I was already so stressed and frazzled, so I couldn't even stop to grieve. We took our sweet Smush to the vet to be cremated, cried as we held him, and had to immediately resume packing. I hoped their prayers and kindness would help me get through the next few days.

The least helpful and most painful response I received was," Are you going to get another one?" It's just not simple. My sweet Mr. Smushyface could have been mistaken for a stuffed animal—his adorableness was surreal and unrivaled. His sweet, smushed Himalayan face would be waiting for me each morning outside my bedroom door. After pets and scratches (and possibly hugs), he would follow me and wait while I made my coffee, demanding more pets the whole time and almost killing me as he walked in zig-zags in front of my half-awake self.

Then, as I headed for my coffee-drinking spot, he would race into the living room, jump up on the coffee table and wait for me to sit and place a pillow on my lap—and that's where he would sit and receive all his morning pets and scratches and love. We did this every morning. Each time we dispensed ice from the refrigerator, he would fly across the house to sit and wait for his "ice friends" to fall at the sound of the first cube falling. Ice friends are exactly what they sound like—tiny friends made of ice you can bop around the kitchen until they melt, leaving you utterly confused in your kitty brain. And in the most ludicrous act of cuteness, he played patty cake with his brother, Squishy. They'd sit on their haunches across from each other and touch paws over and over like patty-cake until, inevitably, one of them fell over. We called it kitty-cake. Furry family members are not replaceable. While, yes, I may adopt another cat—no, getting another ice-friend-bopping, patty-cake-playing morning kitty is impossible. There is no other Smushy in the whole world. The most helpful and loving responses were full of empathy. Friends called, and I could hear they were choked up with sadness, or their text messages conveyed a deep connection with the grief they knew I was feeling. One friend made a few meals and brought them over to our house to love us in an incredibly practical way.

The other experience that comes to mind is when I had to put down our little Lhasa Apso, Emmie. Emmie was one of two sisters we adopted the month after we got married, so Emmie and Romie helped us start our life together. After 12 years of snuggles, playing, and wearing bows in her long caramel-colored bangs to keep them out of her eyes, Emmie was suddenly diagnosed with chronic obstructive pulmonary disease (COPD). She struggled to breathe, and we were forced to let her go.

I had never considered the decision of burial or cremation, and for some reason, the idea of cremating her struck me as violent and disturbing. Then, as I was wrestling with this gruesome practicality, a friend called to convey her sympathy and immediately began sharing about a relative she'd lost in a horrific bus accident years before. When we hung up, I felt a thousand times worse after she'd vomited the details of her aunt's brutal death. I think it was her way of trying to let me know she understood loss and to connect with the grief I was experiencing. But vomiting her pain onto me when I was already distraught with grief and the shock of loss left me feeling even more overwhelmed with sadness and like I had to take care of and empathize with her as she told her story. I didn't have it to give, and the conversation left me depleted.

The most helpful responses were:

A friend brought me movies to watch and some thoughtful little gifts just to let me know she was thinking of me. When she came over, she just sat with me and let me cry and talk about Emmie. Tears filled her eyes, and I felt her deep compassion and sadness for my loss.

A friend who called and listened to me process my feelings about cremating our sweet Emmie. He helped me think about it in a practical way. He said, "Well, knowing you and how much you love animals, you're probably going to have lots of furry family members through the years." And gently, he added, "It doesn't seem very practical to bury them all in your backyard, and with a sweet touch of humor, I mean, you probably don't want a pet cemetery back there, right?" I laughed because it was so true, and this truth, shared so gently, alleviated my hesitation. I was able to go ahead with cremation, and we received her ashes in a lovely wooden box

> with her name engraved on the side. He was right. Having a full-fledged pet cemetery was absurd and comical, even in a difficult moment. We don't always know what to say when someone is experiencing a loss. I have felt this way myself at times. The friends who have been most helpful to me in my times of grief have been wonderful listeners; they've celebrated the memory of my pet with me, listening to my stories of the funny, sweet things they did—all the things I will miss. They allowed themselves to feel my sadness with me. Maybe they simply expressed they were so sorry for my loss and let me know they were available if I wanted to talk or get out of the house. Sometimes they made meals for us. They didn't make any of my pain or sadness go away, and that's okay. Their kindness made my grief feel just a bit lighter, even for a few moments, and is truly a gift.

HOPE IN GRIEVING A PET

Even if you can't relate, please don't forget to offer support to someone who's lost a pet. It's heartbreaking for many of us when a beloved pet dies. The words "you can get another one" are not comforting. The person knows they can get another one and, in their time, they will make their choice. But another pet is not a replacement for the one lost.

Although another dog, cat, rabbit, horse, etc., can't replace our lost pet, we may find joy and love in the next pet if we choose to get one.

PART FOUR

HOW TO SUPPORT A GRIEVING PERSON

CHAPTER 23

THE NUMBER ONE THING TO REMEMBER

If I had to summarize part four of this book into four words, they would be: "It's not about you." There are two ways to interpret this:

First, It's not about you, your loss, your memories, your grief, your stories. Focus on the other person.

This isn't always easy to do. We automatically think of our similar situations when faced with someone else's loss. I do it; most people do. There will be a point in time when your stories may be of help, but in the early stages of grief, try to keep 100 percent of your attention on the other person and their loss.

Take a moment to put yourself in the griever's shoes. Imagine losing your best friend, someone you've known since you were a kid. The loss is significant, and you're devastated. If Someone you know comes up to you and says, "How are you doing?" You say, "Well, I just lost my best friend to cancer. It's been difficult...". Then they say, "I know how you feel; I lost a friend to cancer last year. He was forty-nine years old and had liver cancer. We have known each other for ten years. He had a wife and young kids. It really tore me up inside. I miss him."

How do you feel after the conversation? Do you feel they've acknowledged your loss? When you hear the other person's story, do you comfort them, even though you are the one who is in the early stages of grief? Do you feel they care about your loss? Are you feeling better or worse after hearing about their friend? My guess is the conversation didn't help you feel better, and you may have felt hurt, angry, or both.

Ten minutes later, you run into someone else, and upon hearing of your loss, they say, "Oh, I'm so sorry to hear of your loss. You must be hurting. Losing someone you've known all your life and were so close to is devastating. What was their name? I'm sorry you lost (name). Sometimes it helps to talk, so please know I want to hear from you if you want to share."

The person who shared their story may care just as much, but it didn't come across that way. Maybe out of nervousness or not knowing a better way to communicate, they compared their grief to yours. When this happens to me, I feel unheard and dismissed. On the other hand, person two probably left you feeling cared for after they acknowledged your loss and grief.

Second, the positive side of "It's not about you" is that any negative reaction from the griever shouldn't be taken personally. This makes approaching the grieving person less intimidating. You can express your grief and let go of the outcome because it's not about you. Everyone is different; there's no one size fits all. There will be people who don't appreciate your attempt at comforting them and don't like questions about their loss. Or maybe they're having a bad day. If they seem upset or offended, you know it's not about you. It's about their grief. You can try again later. Even if they don't respond positively, you've let them know their grief matters.

When someone you know loses a loved one, focus on their loss without bringing up your own. Maybe later it will be appropriate to share your experience to let them know you know what they feel like, but early grief is not the time. Keeping the griever in mind is the most important thing.

Realizing it's not about you will help you get out of your comfort zone. It may take some practice since this is a natural response for many of us. If you catch yourself sharing your story rather than focusing on theirs, don't fret. Change the course of the conversation back to them. Eventually, it will be second nature. All of us need to feel heard. You will give them a gift by thinking of the other person rather than yourself.

CHAPTER 24
HELP IN EARLY GRIEF

I share the following questions because they take a burden from the griever in the first few weeks/months. Early on, the griever may be overwhelmed with emotions and not know what they need. I suggest calling or texting the griever often to check-in. Here are some ideas of what to say or do:

- Do you feel like talking? I'd love to listen to anything you want to say.
- What's on your calendar this week? Can I drive you to any appointments?
- Can I come over today and do a little housecleaning for you?
- Do you need any yard work taken care of?
- Can I take your kids to the park (or movies or out to eat) so you can rest?
- I can't imagine how hard this is for you. Don't forget I'm here for you and want to listen.

- I'm heading to the grocery store. What can I get you? Are you running low on anything (mention some common items)?
- How are your pets doing? Do they need a trip to the dog park or groomer?
- Are there any phone calls I can make for you?
- I'm bringing you a meal tonight. Do you prefer a casserole or a DoorDash gift card?
- Can I help with any paperwork you need doing?
- Do you feel like taking a short walk or a drive?
- If you don't feel like being alone but don't feel like talking, I can just hang out there and be in the next room in case you need me.
- Do you want me to go with you to the cemetery for a visit?
- I know it's soon, but the movie you wanted to see is out. Are you up for it? (Some people may see this as a welcome diversion, but some won't be up for it)
- When you get the ashes back, do you want me to be there when you open them? (Anthony's grandmother asked me to open his, she didn't want to see them, as it was too painful for her).

Keep in mind elderly people are vulnerable if they live alone and have lost their spouse. Paying special attention to them and insisting on helping may keep an elderly person eating and going to appointments.

Don't forget to acknowledge siblings in the aftermath of a child's death. Be sure to call or text them, too, if you know them. If they are young, consider bringing them a stuffed animal or an age-appropriate book on grief. To protect their parents, some siblings avoid talking about their grief in front of them. If they are pre-teen or older, give them an opportunity to talk to you alone so they feel freer to express themselves.

If calling or texting would be an intrusion, send a card in the mail. Not necessarily a sympathy card; it lets them know you're still thinking of them in the weeks and months since the loss. Even if you don't know the person well, this will touch them.

Recently, I spoke with someone who had just lost her husband. She was surprised by the people from her past (elementary school and beyond) who sent her messages or called. So, even if time has passed, let someone know you're aware of their loss and offer your condolences.

One of the best gifts you can give a grieving person is a picture or a video of the deceased person. Share any photos you have. There will never be a new one taken, so even if it's an old photo, it will be a treasure to their family. Keven and Anthony's friends still send photos if they run into one on their phones, and it's always a highlight of my day.

If you know the person well, you'll have a general idea of what they may or may not appreciate. When Anthony died, his grandfather asked his grandmother to remove all the photos of Anthony from the home because it hurt him to look at them. Every griever is different, so it's good to ask beforehand if you're unsure.

The thought of giving a "grief gift" never crossed my mind before I received a few myself. Several people sent me gifts after I lost Keven. The gesture surprised and touched me. One gift I received was a beautiful wind chime that had a wooden heart at the bottom carved with "Listen to the Wind and Know I am Here" and "I Will Always Be With You, Keven" on the other. I sent the same gift to someone who lost her son about a year after I lost Kev. She appreciated it.

I received other meaningful gifts as well: an angel candle holder, a few books on grief, a figurine of an angel, two blankets with pictures of Keven on them, a tapestry with his name and dates on it, and a lovely necklace with a bird flying free out of a cage with Kev's birthstone. Gifts like these last a lifetime, and I think of the person who gave each one to me every time I use or see it.

In early and late grief, text or call the griever if you have a good memory about their loved one. I'll never forget a text I got from Ross, Keven's best friend. It was a photo of a turntable playing a Smashing Pumpkins album, and sitting right next to it was the little jar of Keven's ashes I had given him. No words are needed. I was so touched. I knew exactly what he was saying with the photo. "I'm thinking of Kev as I listen to one of his favorite bands on the turntable he gave me, and he's here with me," Ross said.

When my father died, he left behind two sisters and six brothers. Several of them made it a regular habit to call my mom once a week and check on her. I know it meant the world to her to hear from them. One uncle would come to visit every week or two in the beginning. He'd rotate turns taking each of us kids out to dinner alone. It was the next best thing to my dad being alive. It was his way of letting us know he loved us and was there for us whenever we needed him. Aunts and uncles, brothers and sisters-in-law can be an enormous source of comfort for children and adults alike.

With child loss, I know many parents who've stayed close to their child's friends. Anthony had a lot of friends and left behind nine who helped me get through the first year. I'm still close to most of them. Keven had several close friends at the time of his death. His three best friends from his childhood visit me when they are in the area, text me, and even had a portrait painted for me of the four of them together (it hangs in the front room for all to see). I love those young men. They remind me of the best days of Keven's life.

In early grief, it's tough for most of us to think clearly. If the loss is someone in our immediate family, we become easily overwhelmed with the "to-do list" that follows a death. It is much more helpful to make suggestions instead of asking, "What can I do for you?" You will make a genuine difference to the griever by alleviating them of some tasks.

Grievers, early grief will eventually evolve into forever grief. Then, it will be easier to breathe, think, and live again. Do whatever you need to do in the beginning that helps you through the day. You will survive, even though it may seem impossible at the time.

CHAPTER 25

BIRTHDAYS, HOLIDAYS, MEMORIAL DATES

Certain dates on the calendar become almost unbearable after a significant loss. For me, two of those are Keven and Anthony's memorial dates, August 11 and September 15. Months in advance, I start dreading those dates. There's more pain in the weeks leading up to them than on the actual date because the anticipation lasts ten times as long as the day itself.

As soon as someone you care about loses a loved one, mark the date on your calendar along with their birthday and have it repeat every year. I promise you, letting their family know you remember these dates will speak volumes about how much you care. Even if you don't know the family well, you can find them on social media and drop them a message; it will make an unbearable day less painful.

All holidays are exceptionally difficult the first year after a loss and continue to be for those closest to their loved ones. It hurts when it seems like everyone forgets you're missing someone significant. Valentine's Day, Thanksgiving, Hanukkah, Christmas, and the 4th of July are never the same again. It magnifies the loss when the whole family gathers, but your loved one seems forgotten.

My family rarely brings up Keven. I understand it's awkward for them, they don't want to say the wrong thing, and they aren't sure what the right thing is. I'm "training" them to know I want them to mention him. The first year I was so hurt that no one said a word at Thanksgiving, but then I realized they probably thought it would upset me, so I bring him up every time we are together. I hope this opens the door for his cousins to talk about him more. When they share, I hear funny stories about his childhood I never knew before.

It takes bravery to do this; remember, it's not about you. You can say something as simple as "I think of John often and miss him too." Of course, everyone is different, and you may know someone is uncomfortable talking about their loved one, but most of us long for it. So what can you do or say on your holiday to acknowledge the grievers in your life?

What else could you say on these occasions? Acknowledge the missing person with an upbeat memory or comment, "Grandpa used to love carving the turkey," or "Mom would enjoy this." "Remember how excited he used to get to watch fireworks?" "She gave the greatest gifts."

The simple expression "I miss him/her too" helps soothe the grieving person's broken heart and hopefully will loosen up any tension about the obvious empty chair at the table. Some families continue setting a place at the table for the missing person. If you host a holiday, try to find out if it would bring comfort or tears.

It's easy to recognize birthdays with a phone call or text. My closest friends remember Keven's birthday each year by saying, "I know it's his birthday today; I'm thinking of you." That's all you need to say; it's simple. Knowing they remember makes a tremendous difference. It says to me they care about me and Kev. Keven and Anthony's friends do a good job of keeping in touch with me on their birthdays and memorial dates, and I love it. The thought of someone you love being forgotten is painful, especially on their birthday.

Lighting a candle in their memory is also a thoughtful gesture. You can take a picture of the candle and text it to the griever with a note, "This is for your mom on her memorial date."

A friend told me one of her friends planted a tree to honor her husband after he passed. Each year, the friend sends her a photo to show the tree's growth as a reminder she's thinking of her on that date.

The memorial anniversary is usually the toughest day of the year for the griever. It's still alive in their memories, and having it acknowledged is a very thoughtful gesture. Ask if they have plans to do anything in remembrance of their lost loved one. If not, ask them if they'd like to plan something. It can be as simple as visiting a gravesite, going out to eat at their favorite restaurant, or getting a group together to share stories.

Some people like to release balloons which is a nice thought but not good for wildlife or the environment and has become illegal in some places. Instead, consider "Wishing Lanterns". They are eco-friendly, biodegradable, and affordable. They are beautiful as they float peacefully up into the sky and can be written on like balloons.

The first year after losing Keven, I had wristbands made in black with white lettering. One side said, "Keven Legere," and the opposite side said, "Never Forgotten." I sent them to his closest friends, his cousins, and a few of my close friends, asking them to wear them twice a year to remember Kev. Now I get text photos of them wearing the bracelets twice a year. Wristbands are inexpensive, so it's another idea to consider offering them to a friend.

This year, I was going to invite some friends to watch his memorial video with me via Zoom. He passed at the height of the COVID-19 pandemic, so only a few people could attend his service. But as the date approached, I was too nervous to invite anyone. I felt awkward initiating it because I didn't want anyone to feel uncomfortable or obligated—more reason to remind yourself of these dates and offer these ideas to the grieving person. You can be creative and come up with ways to recognize these significant days throughout the years. Sending photos or videos to the family will be like presenting them with a gift of love. If you know your friend's mom, dad, or siblings, please stay in touch with them. So many moms I know love having their son or daughter's friends still in their lives. It's a beautiful gift; you often have stories or old photos we never knew about, and sharing them is like bringing the loved one back to life for a few minutes.

CHAPTER 26

CLICHÉS ARE GENERALLY UNHELPFUL

This chapter is the heart of the book. If you're thumbing through, stop here for "the basics."

There will always be people who don't know how to respond to grief with compassion and empathy. There will be people who say the wrong things, talk about themselves, or ignore your loss completely. You can be fairly confident that your condolences will be appreciated if you follow these guidelines.

Our culture avoids talking about death, so we rely on these clichés; some of these statements are more harmful than helpful.

Grievers, please safeguard yourself by being prepared for insensitive comments and unrealistic expectations. Try to stay away from negative people. Hopefully, compassion will be better communicated someday.

When communicating with a griever, don't start sentences with "you should" or "at least." There's some truth to some of these statements, but not in the early stages of grief when the focus should be on the heartache of the loss.

COMMON "YOU SHOULD" STATEMENTS TO AVOID

- You should have seen it coming.
- You should eat something.
- You should be thankful you have more kids.
- You should feel better by now.
- You should be thankful; it could have been worse.
- You should get out more.
- You should try yoga or meditation.
- You should get some rest.
- You should see a therapist.
- You should be thankful it was painless.
- You should put on a cheerful face around the kids.

A time will come when yoga, meditation, and therapy can be suggested. But, unless the loss debilitates the person and needs immediate help from a doctor or therapist, wait a few months.

I'm sorry for your loss (is fine for most people)
"I'm sorry for your loss" is the number one thing we say when we hear someone we know has experienced a death. Most people accept this as it's intended, but not everyone does. Some people dislike hearing "I'm sorry for your loss" because they think of being sorry as an apology (which is one definition).

The other day I heard a woman saying how much she hated hearing it when she lost her husband. "Why are they telling me they're sorry? It's not their fault!" She was pretty adamant about it. But "sorry" has more than one definition. When we say, "I'm sorry for your loss," the meaning is "being grieved or saddened." Another way to think of this definition is, "Your loss makes me sad for you and grieves me too," which I believe to be very appropriate.

I know how you feel (comparing grief, again, it's not about you)

We talked about this earlier, but it's worthy of a reminder. This could be one of the least comforting things to say and do. I'll even go as far as saying it will piss some people off, and rightly so.

If we compare our grief to theirs, we're not focused on the grieving person. It's human nature to be reminded of our own grief when we hear of a similar loss. But this is not our moment—this is not the time to tell someone who lost his wife to cancer you lost your mom to cancer and go into a story about it.

What if you, too, have lost your wife to cancer? You can say something like, "I lost my wife to cancer also, so I have *an idea* how much you're hurting." Other moms who've experienced losing a child to suicide or overdose have said this to me. I find it comforting because I know they get it, and I'm not alone. I try never to say, "I know how you feel." This doesn't need much explanation, but here are a few examples:

A woman in a grief group told another mom: "I know how you feel; I saw someone killed in a car accident" when she learned her daughter died from COVID-19. What? This makes no sense at all. The person saying it isn't thinking about you and your loss; they are thinking about their own unrelated experience.

Another mom had someone compare her son's loss to a dog's. Now, I love dogs, and mine are my "babies." Losing a beloved pet is heart-wrenching. It carries its own special type of grief. But to compare a dog to a human son is beyond insensitive; it's insulting.

A guy I know told me when his father died, someone immediately went into a long story about how he lost his mother at a young age and how it traumatized his life. This happens more than you might think. We are uncomfortable, so we try to take the focus off the death, but in doing so, we come across as uncaring and insensitive.

At the end of the book, I've listed outrageous things people have said to a grieving person, and there are a few on the list that will blow your mind. I share them to entertain you and illuminate how condolences don't always come across right if we don't know what to say.

God wanted him home

A group of sayings fall under the category of God/heaven/angels. Even if these statements are true, they don't bring comfort. If you're not 100 percent certain the other person has the same spiritual beliefs as you, avoid the topic altogether. Even for someone who believes in God, heaven, and the afterlife, these statements come across as "you shouldn't feel so bad; look at the bright side."

- God needed another angel, so he took her home.
- He's in heaven now.
- God's timing is perfect. It was her time.
- God knows what he's doing, don't question him.
- God needed him more than you do.
- God never gives you more than you can handle.
- God will provide for you and take away your pain.
- You'll see him again in heaven.
- Now you have an angel watching over you.
- It's God's will.
- She's in a better place.

Rather than trying to justify the loss, acknowledge that

death is devastating and heartbreaking. We all mean well when we make these statements; we care and want to make the griever feel better. However, from what I've experienced and learned from others, acknowledging the grief by saying, "You must be devastated; I don't know what to say, but I care about what you're going through" or "I can't imagine what kind of pain you're in, I wish I could take some of it away" is more helpful than the above statements.

After Keven died, someone told me God needed him home, and he wasn't meant to live for over 29 years. It made me feel worse. I wanted to say, "You're wrong! I need him more than God does. How dare God take my only child." but I kept silent and chalked it up to another case of people having good intentions but no clue what to say.

Get over it (unrealistic expectations)

As I mentioned, three months after I lost Keven, someone told me I needed to "snap out of it." I was shocked, but I knew he was really saying, "It hurts me to see you suffering like this. I want you to feel good, not bad." Still, an inappropriate thing to say, but he didn't know any better. He'd never lost a child. Please keep in mind everyone grieves differently. Moving from the initial devastation of a loss to coping and moving on takes time. It may take one person a year to want to socialize again, another only a few months or less. We're all unique, and that's a good thing.

NOTE TO GRIEVERS:

It can feel like we're not honoring our loved ones if we go out and have fun too soon. Sometimes, in the beginning, I felt guilty for laughing. Yet, I believe Keven and Anthony want me to be happy, to laugh, and enjoy life as best as I can. It may take a while to get to the point of fun again, but you will get there. We never completely get over our grief, it changes over time, and it's not something to "put an end to."

They're no longer suffering

It seems harmless when you're talking about someone who has endured a long illness or is being tortured by their own thoughts like Keven was. There are times when this statement is true. In early grief, maybe the deceased isn't suffering anymore, but the griever is.

I believe in an afterlife and don't believe there's suffering there. Not everyone shares that view. There are so many beliefs about what happens to us after we die; saying this to someone who doesn't believe in an afterlife can be upsetting.

Like the "God" statements above, these words didn't provide me any comfort in early grief even though I believed it to be true. It's another phrase that avoids and minimizes grief by suggesting the griever should look at the "bright side."

Grief isn't about the person who died; it's about the person left behind who misses their loved one and can't imagine life without them.

I'm here for you (then abandonment)

After the first few weeks, condolences slow down. The cards and flowers stop arriving. There are fewer phone calls and messages. Initially, you will receive a great deal of sympathy from family and friends, but this will fade out in time, with only those closest to you checking in on you. This feels like we've been abandoned, which is often the case. When people stop caring or don't realize you are still grieving, it hurts. It can leave a person feeling lonely or even resentful.

For many of us, this is when we need a friend the most. The numbness has worn off. If the loss was someone exceptionally close, a spouse, child, sibling, or best friend, our entire lives have changed. Now we realize how uncomfortable people are around us. Grievers don't want to burden anyone, so they stay silent and feel alone.

As the weeks pass, many will drift away for a variety of reasons:

1. They don't stop caring; they just don't realize you still need them.
2. Your loss causes them to feel uncomfortable, so they desert you.
3. They avoid you as much as possible because they are tired of hearing about your loss.
4. They get impatient waiting for your old self to return and become the same person you were before your loss (you may never be the same, so if they can't accept the new you, they probably aren't your best friend).
5. It reminds them they could lose someone, and they prefer to avoid thinking about it.

It takes a dedicated friend to listen empathetically and encourage someone to share their feelings. Be sure to check in often at first and remember to be there for them as time goes on. You can show them you're there for them by:

- Simply sending an "I'm thinking of you" text message.
- Saying you would enjoy seeing photo albums of their lost loved one. (Seeing old photos may be too painful for some grievers, but for others, it's comforting.)

- Show them you're one of those people who'll stick around because you want to listen and can handle uncomfortable things.
- Stay in communication with them, asking them what will help them at that moment or making suggestions.

It's important to understand grief never goes away; it just changes. It has taken me some time to adjust to my new "normal," but Keven remains in my heart and in my mind every second of every day. It's something that envelops me, even if I am not consciously thinking of him. Let go of expectations. Everyone is different.

Your words matter and give you the ability to offer genuine support to someone in grief. Body language and facial expression also matter. Keep an eye on your facial expression to see if it's one of sympathy or discomfort. Do you know this person will accept a hug? If not, take their hand in yours and look into their eyes as you express your sympathy for their loss and offer to do something specific to help or ask if they'd like to talk. Comparing grief or saying, "I know how you feel," both dismiss the person's loss. We can't know how someone else feels, but if we've had a very similar loss, we'll have an idea of how they feel, which can bring comfort a bit later in grief.

Losing a loved one can be the most traumatizing event of a person's life. Being surrounded by people who understand and sincerely care helps the healing process. If you say something "wrong," remember, it's been ingrained in our heads for years. Don't feel bad; just remember to pick different words next time. When you say something that brings comfort, your words will be appreciated and remembered.

What will you do now?

As I wrote this chapter, my sister received a call from her best friend, Denise. Denise lost her fifty-three-year-old husband unexpectedly to a heart attack. I'm in shock as my fingers hit the keyboard. It was completely unexpected. He left behind two children, 19 and 15, and was the main financial supporter of the family. Naturally, one of the first things my sister and I thought was, "How is she going to get by without Rob?" This thought crosses our minds because we care and worry about the future of our friends. It can be overwhelming for the griever to hear your concerns right now. There's a combination of numbness and devastation that seems to happen at the same time. Asking this question too early could be the tipping point for someone who hasn't had time to process. There's nothing wrong with this question if asked by a very close friend, but timing is everything.

Just listen (a true gift)

Listening is a gift. It's not always easy to listen, especially to someone who's hurting, but I've found offering the gift of listening is rewarding for both people. It's very similar to giving a physical gift, something you picked out knowing your friend would love it, then seeing the joy in their eyes when they receive it. You feel good because of it.

Listening is a skill anyone can learn. Here are a few thoughts on how to hone your listening skills:

- Focus on supporting the griever, nothing else. It may feel uncomfortable at first. You may be tempted to change the subject or to talk about yourself. Guard against by putting yourself in the other person's shoes and imagining how it would feel if they suddenly started talking about a different topic when you're in the middle of sharing.

- Ask questions that require more than a "yes" or "no" answer. This will not only show the griever you're paying attention, but it can help them process what they are feeling and thinking. It allows the griever to feel heard when you show you're focusing on their words.
- Look at the person as they speak. Looking around while they're talking says, "I'm bored," and can be very hurtful.

I'll never forget when my friend, Virginia, asked me out to coffee about a year after Keven's death. We hadn't seen each other since the memorial service. After grabbing our drinks, she said, "So, talk to me. I want to hear everything about Keven, your grief, whatever you feel like sharing." Then she sat there and listened, occasionally asking a question, or adding her memories of Kev, but never once taking her eyes off me or changing the topic. We laughed, we cried, and afterward, I felt a lightness I hadn't felt in a long time.

Time heals all wounds (not really, but it helps)

Broken hearts don't heal with time. Even though time takes the edge off our emotional wounds and grief, it doesn't go back to normal. Time heals physical wounds, but even then, there can be leftover scars and pain. Over a year ago, I fell flat on my face on a cement patio. Besides suffering a traumatic brain injury and a concussion, I also fractured my orbital bone, bit through my lip, and had a deep cut above my eyebrow, which required 20 stitches. The scars on my face aren't as noticeable now, but the lingering effects of the head injury are still with me and, according to my doctor, always will be (vertigo, huge floaters in my vision, and short-term memory issues.)

The pain of the fall is gone, but the scars remind me of it every time I look in the mirror. The scars from grief will never leave us, even if we seem happy and like we've moved on and healed. Once again, using "time heals all wounds" avoids recognizing the real issues - the pain of loss, and the sorrow in the heart of loved ones. For me, I didn't want to be reminded that things would be "better" in the future. My life was forever changed when Keven died, and it devastated me. Part of me thought that the world should stop turning due to this tragic event. Nothing would ever be the same again. Running errands, I wondered how anyone could smile—my son was dead. Of course, they did not know. It's not a rational thought, but it *feels* that way in the beginning.

How are you doing? (do you honestly want to know?)

This is a sincere question and totally appropriate to ask. When approached with this question, the griever has a choice to make, "Should I tell them how I really feel, or should I just say I'm getting by?"

When asked by a close family member or friend, someone we feel safe with, we may let it all out. But if we're in a public place or asked by someone we don't have a close relationship with, we usually lie to avoid creating an awkward situation. I learned this the hard way while grocery shopping.

If it's early grief, assume we're not doing well and instead offer to listen by saying something like this, "You're going through a major loss; you must feel so many emotions. I'd love to listen if you want to share." Then listen without interrupting, without trying to lessen the pain or "fix it." This is one of those times where you should give 100% of your attention to the griever. If your mind is wandering while they're talking, they will notice your facial expression and feel even worse by your lack of sincerity.

If you're not the type of person who can sit and listen to someone's deep pain, it is perfectly fine. Instead of offering to listen, do something that comes more naturally to you, like providing them a service or sharing memories of their loved one.

What can I do for you? (actions speak louder than words)

People who genuinely care and want to show support ask, "What can I do to help?" or "Let me know what you need." On the surface, this seems generous and kind because it is! Most grievers can't think in early grief. It's hard even to remember the first few days after losing Keven. I was in a fog; nothing seemed real to me. I didn't know what my needs were.

In early grief, the emotions are on overload, and there's a long list of things that must happen right away. So rather than putting the griever on the spot to come up with something, it's more helpful to offer to do specific things, which I will discuss in a moment. First, I want to share an example of what actionable support in early grief looks like. I was very fortunate in early grief because my then-boyfriend, Peter, immediately drove seven hours to be by my side. He quietly took care of everything and allowed me to do whatever I needed to do: cry, respond to messages, curl up in a ball, and stare into space. If I needed a hug, he was there. If I needed to be alone, he understood.

He'd known Keven for four years and was grieving too, but he put my needs first. The smallest things seemed overwhelming to me. Peter took care of the day-to-day for my sister and me, cleaning, cooking, shopping, the pets, and so forth. He waited on us, brought us water, gave us hugs, and made sure we ate. He also helped me shop for something to wear, took me to the mortuary, drove Keven's clothes to the mortuary, and helped me pick out music for the memorial video.

Peter had no expectations of me, which I didn't recognize until later. He instinctively knew to "go with the flow." I experienced a hurricane of emotions that were unpredictable and intense. If you know someone in early grief, let them go through the emotions.

Along with Peter, I had several close friends stop by, and some offered to get the flowers with vases for the service; they brought food and paper products and sat and listened to me croak out the story and repeat myself over and over (I had lost my voice because I screamed so much upon finding Keven).

Not all of us have someone like Peter by our side or friends who know just what to do to help. Here are some questions you can ask in the earliest days of grief before a memorial service/funeral:

- Do you need help planning the service or the reception?
- Do you need help writing an obituary or eulogy?
- Do you need me to order flowers, food, etc.?
- Can I drop anything off at the mortuary for you?
- Do you need a guest book? I can get one and receive guests for you.
- Do you need help to create a video montage?
- I have some photos of your loved one. Should I email them to you or drop off hard copies?
- Is there anyone you haven't been able to contact you want to notify? I can do it for you.
- I'm bringing you a meal tonight. Would you prefer a gift card to DoorDash or lasagna? Do you have special nutritional needs/preferences?

- I'm going to drop off some paper plates, cups, and napkins at your house, so you don't have to worry about doing dishes for a while. Should I leave them on the front porch, or are you up for a visit?
- Do you need gas in your car or a car wash? Let me do that for you.
- Is there anything you need picked up at the dry cleaners or pharmacy?

The grieving person may not be thinking of details and will appreciate you for coming up with these offers to help. Some people have a difficult time accepting help. If you know this, be gentle but firm in trying to let them take some of these things off their list and emphasize how much it would mean to you to be of service during this time.

NOTE TO THE GRIEVER:

In the initial days after a loss, friends and extended family want to support you. Let them help. These offers will not last beyond the first few weeks (if that long) so let others assist you. It's as much for them as it is for you. They feel helpless and know they can't take away your pain, so allowing them to bring meals, run errands, do house cleaning, and so forth allows them to express their love in actions and show you how much they care.

They wouldn't want to see you unhappy

The other version, "They would want you to be happy." This statement offers no compassion, empathy, or understanding of what the grieving person is going through, even if it's true. What the grieving person hears is, "You shouldn't be unhappy; the person you lost is upset because you're sad." There are no "you should" in grief. We each feel what we need to feel when we need to feel it. It's painful, it's scary, and there are times you wish you were dead, too, but all those things are necessary to feel in order to move through the never-ending process of grief. If you feel compelled to bring up the lost loved one, use it in a way to provide comfort rather than trying to make the person feel bad for their unhappiness or feel like they are letting their loved one down. Being reminded Keven loves me makes me happy. I know he does, and he knows I love him. I say it in the present tense because I still love him and still feel his love for me. It's okay to remind someone that the love is still there.

You're handling this so well

This is usually said by someone who isn't close to you and hasn't seen you wailing, or cursing, or despondent. The first time this was said to me, I immediately got defensive and said, "Not really, you've never seen me in private." Most likely, it's meant to encourage, but it doesn't feel that way to the griever. As I've mentioned before, we learn to put on our "public face" so we don't draw attention to ourselves or make anyone around us uncomfortable. Early in grief, assume someone is not handling it well. Over time, their grief will evolve. I find the opposite more comforting, "You must be hurting inside even though you seem to handle it well on the outside."

Silence

Silence is good... and bad. Good silence is being there for someone without needing words to convey how much you hurt for them. Allowing the griever to express their grief without trying to make them feel better or "fix it."

Five months before I lost Keven, my dear friend Debbie lost her son Nick. I met Nick a few times, and what stuck out to me was his relationship with his mom (and his gorgeous green eyes).

They were so close. It reminded me of Keven and me. So, when I heard Nick passed, I dropped to my knees in shock. It devastated me. When I went to see Debbie, neither of us said a word. We just stood hugging each other. She could feel what I was "saying" without words. Five months later, she dropped to her knees upon hearing about Keven's death. Our empathy is still in full swing today. We talk about our boys a lot.

The other silence is not acknowledging the loss, no call, card, or visit. Ignoring someone's loss with silence sends a message that you don't care. But what if you do care? What if you're just unsure of what to say or do? The thought of being around them makes you very uncomfortable. Maybe you're afraid of saying the wrong thing or triggering your own grief. That's why I wrote this book, it's not uncommon to feel that way.

It's difficult for some of us to express how hurt we are to see someone we care about suffering in grief. Do your best. Send a card or text if you can't bear to speak to the person—it's perfectly fine; however, it's not fine to ignore the loss. Don't let your own tears keep you away. Tears are a form of communicating how much you care. Let them flow. When someone cries with me, I feel their empathy 100 percent.

You must be over your grief. You're having too much fun to be grieving

Something I saw recently prompted me to include it here. A friend in my support group, "Sue," posted something on social media this week that immediately put me on the defensive. Sue lost her beloved son several years ago, *and* she enjoys an active and adventurous life. Someone suggested she must not be grieving anymore (or enough) because she posts photos of herself having a good time with friends, and family, traveling, and her passion for music.

The comments she received confirmed I'm alone in my anger.

We all came to her defense and explained that just because someone appears to be having a good time doesn't mean they aren't grieving. Very few people share pictures (or videos) of themselves crying. Very few people post photos of them sitting at home feeling broken. People don't scroll through social media to see sadness and grief.

Is Sue being fake by only posting happy photos of her life? No. She's doing it because she knows like all grieving moms know, people don't want to see our pain and suffering. Society has taught us we should express it in private. She posts to share her life with others, and I always look forward to seeing what she's up to.

Her posts are a beacon of hope, pointing out that even when your heart is shattered, life can be enjoyable.

Be strong/this will make you strong (I'm already strong)

Why do people say this? It's a cliché we've all heard and said without really thinking about it. It makes no sense to tell someone who's grieving to be strong. They should be allowed to just "be." Everyone is different. Some people will try to be strong out of a sense of obligation; a father, for example, trying to protect his children after losing their mother.

Most people are in transition after losing a loved one. One moment they could be fine, the next sobbing. They should feel and do whatever they need to get through each moment.

Another thing to avoid saying when a young child loses a parent is, "You're the man of the house now" or "You need to fill your mother's shoes now." Someone said this to my 12-year-old brother after my father died. I will never forget hearing it. He took it to heart, and it was very unfair to burden a child with this responsibility.

"You'll be stronger because of this," or "You're so strong for getting through this." We have no choice about making it

through; we may look strong on the outside, but inside, we may feel the opposite. I felt lost, unsure of any decision I made, and doubtful I would survive.
People mean well by this statement. When I hear it, I usually think to myself, "*I was already strong long before I lost Anthony or Keven.*" Any parent of an addict that has been in the trenches, watching their child suffer is strong. It's incredibly difficult to endure; it's traumatic and exhausting.

In social situations, people who are in forever grief are used to putting on a happy face so they don't make others uncomfortable. It's easier to pretend than deal with the discomfort of someone quickly changing the subject. We shouldn't feel forced to pretend we're happy, and we damn sure shouldn't have to defend ourselves if we are. I hope this changes.

My hope for everyone who's grieving is to get to the point where they can balance grief and joy and have a fulfilling life. It didn't happen overnight for my friend Sue; it took time. Early grief is full of pain. But even in early grief, we may find ourselves laughing or feeling good for a period of time. Eventually, we should all be as fortunate as Sue. Some of us will, some of us won't. Some of us may have moments of envy or self-pity when we compare our lives to one like hers; it's normal human feelings. But for anyone who thinks we don't deserve to live with joy or thinks it's disrespectful to our deceased loved one, rest assured, we are crying on the inside.

I believe there is an afterlife, and the people we're closest to remain in our lives from that realm. I can imagine Keven hanging out with Sue's son and saying, "Wow, your mom is living her fullest life. That's exactly what I want for my mom too."

CHAPTER 27

FINAL THOUGHTS

After the first few weeks of a loss, things slow down a lot. The cards and flowers stop arriving. There are fewer phone calls and social media messages. The immediate outpouring of sympathy from your closest friends, family, acquaintances, and people from your past fizzles out. But the grief is still so fresh and can leave a person feeling exhausted and alone.

For many of us, this is when we need a friend the most. The numbness wears off. Our entire lives have changed if the loss was someone exceptionally close, a spouse, child, sibling, or best friend. There is a big missing piece of our hearts. We may want to talk about it but don't want to burden anyone.

It takes a special person to sit and listen empathetically and encourage someone to share their feelings. If that's you, be sure to check in often during this time. Ask if they want to talk about it, and let them know you want to listen.

As I mentioned, many will drift away as the weeks go on. It's not because they stop caring; it's usually because they don't realize you still need them. When someone we care about is missing a significant loved one, encourage them to keep talking about their person.

Your words matter and allow you to offer genuine support to someone in grief. Body language and facial expression also matter. Check to see if you're displaying a look of sympathy or discomfort. Do you know this person will accept a hug? If not, take their hand in yours and look into their eyes as you express your sympathy for their loss and offer to do something specific to help or ask if they'd like to talk.

Make sure you address the grieving person and their pain, not the suffering of the one who is no longer here.

Losing a loved one can be the most traumatizing event of a person's life. Being surrounded by people who understand and sincerely care helps the healing process. If you say something "wrong," remember, it's been ingrained in our minds for years. Please don't feel bad; use it as a reminder to choose different words next time. If someone uses a cliché to comfort you, they most likely mean well and don't know what else to say.

When you say something comforting and make gestures of support, you will be appreciated and remembered for helping someone through one of the most painful times of their life.

HOPE FOR THE GRIEVER

Although grief doesn't end, we learn to live within it. We laugh again; we find joy again. Getting through early grief is one of the hardest things many of us ever have to face, but it's possible.

Most things that hurt or anger you are a combination of misunderstanding or an attempt to protect oneself from the painful and scary reality that it could someday be them in your shoes. They mean no harm.

We each have ways of keeping the relationship alive with our loved ones even after death. Some people have special places to feel closer to their loved ones, maybe a gravesite, a place in nature, or a restaurant. We have different ways of celebrating their lives. Mostly for me, I talk to Keven throughout my day and say goodnight to him before I fall asleep.

Living with a hole in your heart is difficult, but it's possible. We go on. Some days we want to die to escape the agony of the loss. Sometimes the pain is so unbearable we think we're going to die. Some days we feel pretty good, and other days we feel great. No matter what, we get up every morning and do it again. We get better at it as time goes on. We can socialize again, dance again, fall in love, give of ourselves, laugh, and enjoy life. Even though Keven's absence is a hole that will never heal, his memory is a blessing that fills me with warmth.

Keven and Anthony are gone from my physical world, but they're still very much a part of my life. I can hear their voices sometimes, floating through time and space, saying, "I love you, Mom." My Anthony memories are usually when I'm in my car. We spent a lot of time together driving. He had a great voice and knew the lyrics to many songs, even my classic rock genre. He sent me a specific sign once as I drove, reminding me he would always be with me. "Firework" by Katy Perry never fails to bring a huge Anthony smile to my face. He loved singing that one.

Often when I do something Keven and I did together (like watching certain TV shows), I remember exactly what he said or how his laugh sounded. He's also alive in my thoughts and my sister's. We often joke about what Kev would say if he were still here because we know him so well. But he's still my baby, my boy, my son. He will always be at the center of my life.

We don't have to grieve alone. There is someone out there

willing to listen. Loss can bring people together that would otherwise have nothing in common.

This quote comforts me; I hope it helps you as well:

"Death ends a life, not a relationship." (From *Tuesdays With Morrie* by Mitch Albom.)

PART FIVE

100 INAPPROPRIATE & OUTRAGEOUS COMMENTS

CHAPTER 1
100 INAPPROPRIATE & OUTRAGEOUS COMMENTS

Most of us have said some of these things on this list. I know I have before I knew better. There's no judgment here. For years, we've been conditioned.

All of these statements are real!

I asked several groups of people to share with me the most inappropriate or outrageous thing that was said to them after they lost a loved one. My hope is this book has shown alternatives. But as you will see, some of these statements are downright insensitive and ridiculous.

1. Are you sad about this, or is it a relief they're gone?
2. Are you over this yet? (after a few months)
3. At least she made it to old age.
4. At least one twin lived.
5. At least you have memories.
6. At least you have more children.
7. Be grateful for the children you still have.
8. Can I rent your extra room now that he's gone?

9. Cremating him means he won't get into heaven.
10. Do you have an insurance policy for her? How much?
11. Don't be a buzzkill (after a mother brings up her child in a group of "friends")
12. Don't cry.
13. Don't let this get you down. Death is part of life.
14. Don't bring it up so often; people will start avoiding you, including me.
15. Do you think she made it to heaven?
16. Did you expect them to get better? (after a long illness)
17. Everyone's hoping you'll get over this soon.
18. Everything happens for a reason.
19. God knows what he's doing. Don't question it.
20. God needed another angel.
21. God needed him more than you do.
22. God never gives you more than you can handle.
23. How could you let her be cremated?
24. How could you let his body be buried underground, covered in dirt?
25. How long will you be grieving?
26. I forgive you for being so depressed about this.
27. I thought you'd be over it by now.
28. I'd have killed myself if I went through everything you went through.
29. I'd like to hang out with you, but only on a day you're not mourning.
30. I'll check in on you, and we'll get together (then never call).
31. I'm praying for her soul.
32. I'm praying for you. (this one comforts some, but not all)

33. If a cop killed him, he must have been doing something wrong.
34. If I were you, I'd feel so hopeless and lost.
35. I knew this would happen to him. He was asking for it.
36. It probably doesn't even phase you anymore after losing so many people.
37. It was only a dog/cat; you can get another one.
38. It wasn't a baby yet (to a woman after a miscarriage).
39. It's been three months. Maybe you're not grieving the right way.
40. It's the same as getting a divorce.
41. It's time to move on from feeling sorry for yourself.
42. It's selfish to grieve for this long; think of everyone else.
43. I've always loved her red dress. Can I have it?
44. I've lost more people than you have.
45. Let me know when you're ready to date again. I've always had a thing for you.
46. Literally, everyone dies eventually.
47. Losing your son must be like when I had my appendix removed.
48. Man up! Men don't cry.
49. Now you have an angel looking over you.
50. Now you will appreciate life so much more.
51. People die all the time; it's natural.
52. Praise God! She's in heaven now!
53. Rather than taking care of a disabled child/parent, you can live your own life now.
54. Regarding suicide death: Obviously, it's what she wanted.
55. She brought in on herself.

56. Should I invite you to my party? Or are you still acting sad all the time?
57. Snap out of it.
58. So many of your friends have died. You'll be joining them again soon. (to an elderly person)
59. Sorry, I didn't go to the funeral. I forgot what date it was.
60. Sorry, I didn't invite you out with us; I knew you wouldn't want to go.
61. Stay busy and try not to think about it.
62. Stay positive!
63. Stop crying!
64. Suicide is selfish.
65. Time heals all wounds.
66. The funeral went on too long.
67. There are so many people who have it worse than this.
68. Think of all the money you'll save on food. She ate so much.
69. This, too, shall pass.
70. To a young boy, "You're the man of the house now."
71. Use affirmations daily. It will help.
72. Was he saved? If not, he's in hell.
73. We miss the old you. When will she be back?
74. What a horrifying way to die. He must have been in so much pain!
75. What are you doing with their belongings? Maybe there's something I want.
76. What will you be serving at the reception?
77. When talking about your loved one: can we change the subject?
78. When you get back to the office, I don't want this to interfere with your work.

79. Who wrote the obituary? It wasn't very good.
80. Why do you still talk about your son?
81. Will "so and so" be at the funeral? If so, I'm not going.
82. You didn't get to know the baby, so it should be easy to get over.
83. You don't seem upset.
84. You have to stay strong.
85. You must be so mad at him (for ending his own life).
86. You need to get used to this. They aren't coming back.
87. You two didn't get along very well; this shouldn't be too upsetting for you.
88. You shouldn't feel this bad.
89. You're no fun anymore.
90. You're strong; you'll get through this.
91. You told me you two had problems. You should be glad he's gone.
92. You weren't together anymore; it makes no sense you're this upset.
93. You're too young to understand genuine grief.
94. You've got so much to be thankful for, don't be sad.
95. You'll be stronger because of this.
96. You'll have so much less stress now that your daughter is gone.
97. You're still attractive; you can meet someone new.
98. You're young enough to have another child.
99. Your parents' death should be a big help to you financially.
100. Your dog was old. Now you can get a puppy and start over.

PART SIX

NEVER FORGET—SAY THEIR NAME

CHAPTER 2

SAY THEIR NAME

Grieving people have a saying: "Say Their Name". When we hear our loved one's name spoken out loud, we know they're not forgotten. I identify most closely with those who've lost someone to suicide or overdose.

This is a list of people who passed from suicide, overdose or fentanyl-laced drugs. They're all loved and missed by someone I know through Solace for Hope or social media. Knowing there are broken hearts behind every name makes it hard to read this list, but this is my way of honoring them by saying their names:

1. Nolan James Smith - Forever 15
2. Christopher Michael Ritchie - Forever 16
3. Noah Gonzalez - Forever 16
4. Mark Melkonian - Forever 17
5. Connor Jack Roberts - Forever 18
6. Kinley Leonard - Forever 18
7. Alexander Joseph Marks - Forever 19

8. Brady Affinito - Forever 19
9. Christopher Joseph Straughn - Forever 19
10. Harley "MOTOE" Swank - Forever 19
11. Jarred Barber - Forever 19
12. Benjamin Dunkle - Forever 20
13. Bryan Terrazas - Forever 20
14. Christopher A. Love - Forever 20
15. Malik Isaiah Dufor - Forever 20
16. Charles Nicholas Vanoff - Forever 20
17. George Pflaumer - Forever 20
18. Casey Thompson - Forever 21
19. Christian Jack Taylor - Forever 21
20. Aaron Sylla - Forever 22
21. Chance Simmons - Forever 22
22. Hailey May Burrell – Forever 22
23. Heather Marie Trott - Forever 22
24. Kaelyn Tomsen - Forever 22
25. Mitchell Craig Fleitman - Forever 22
26. Eric Christopher Pierson - Forever 23
27. Richard C. Maselow - Forever 23
28. Samuel Pantaleon - Forever 23
29. Torin Wood - Forever 23
30. Brandon Tyler Tucker - Forever 24
31. Danny Contreras - Forever 24
32. Mitchell James Sutfin - Forever 24
33. Daniel Donovan Lewis - Forever 25
34. Jayson Garland-Mocnik - Forever 25
35. Justin R. Guittar - Forever 25
36. Lauren Montgomery - Forever 25
37. Ryan David Rapp - Forever 25
38. Tyler Scott Eigelbach - Forever 25
39. Brayce Williams - Forever 26
40. Ethan Jerome Berkowitz - Forever 26

41. Henry Isaac Brown - Forever 26
42. Ian Christopher Jones - Forever 26
43. Ryan Michael Mramer - Forever 26
44. Andrew Alexander D'Paraschi Togo - Forever 27
45. Anthony Maurillo - Forever 27
46. Anthony Edward Pugh - Forever 27
47. Donnie Lace III - Forever 27
48. Jay Phillip Flamm - Forever 27
49. Justin Coffee - Forever 27
50. Justin Michael Logan - Forever 27
51. Mariah Rachel Earp - Forever 27
52. Nicholas Michael Nama - Forever 27
53. Todd Anthony Campbell - Forever 27
54. William (Willie) Aaron-Anthony Ayala - Forever 27
55. Gary Lanigan - Forever 28
56. Riley Alan Ward - Forever 28
57. Ryan Keith Hill - Forever 28
58. Sky Ambruster - Forever 28
59. Tyler Jeremy Terry - Forever 28
60. Alexander Jack Arens - Forever 29
61. Brian Jamison - Forever 29
62. Hunter Anacker - Forever 29
63. Joel Kegan McInnis - Forever 29
64. Justin B.- Forever 29
65. Keven David Legere - Forever 29
66. Scott Austin Cortes - Forever 29
67. Trevor James Manning - Forever 29
68. Autumn Nicole Dawes – Forever 30
69. Darren “Cliff” Piccirillo - Forever 30
70. Davey Herring - Forever 30
71. Joel "Joey" Abraham Cymerint - Forever 30
72. Jordan Varela - Forever 30
73. “Kelly” Y. – Forever 30

74. Kevin Michael Fortin - Forever 30
75. Michael Freeman - Forever 30
76. Noah Naderzad - Forever 30
77. Toby Markes - Forever 30
78. Brian Richard Schickling - Forever 31
79. Christopher Paul Don - Forever 31
80. Shane Eric Hoke - Forever 31
81. Brandon Luke Smith - Forever 32
82. Jessica Anne May - Forever 32
83. Ryan Scott Rapshus - Forever 32.
84. Jessica Griffin Castro – Forever 34
85. Adam Levi Throp - Forever 35
86. Aaron James Lanari (AJ) - Forever 35
87. Beau Bradshaw - Forever 35
88. Jason Richard Paquin – Forever 35
89. Jordan Matthew Rodarte - Forever 35
90. Bryan Berry - Forever 36
91. Nathaniel Craig Hill - Forever 36
92. Adrian Gayle Beaney - Forever 37
93. Fallon Ackerman - Forever 38
94. Damien Robert Repasi - Forever 41
95. Robert Dean Ramsey – Forever 43
96. Alisa Marie Hicks – Forever 44
97. Christopher Lee Bilski – Forever 48
98. Jami Fitzgerald - Forever 54
99. Scott Wilson 54
100. Brent Keith Burrows – Forever 64

BONUS CHAPTERS

BONUS CHAPTER 1
MY BONUS SON ANTHONY

Although Anthony was not my biological son, I loved him as if he were. I refer to him as "the son of my heart" or "my heart son." When Keven and Anthony first met, I tried to convince Kev not to get too close to him when I found out he had a criminal record and was a drug user. However, Keven begged me to give him a chance, promising I'd like Anthony if I got to know him, and he was right!

After spending time together, Anthony and I grew to love one another, and he started calling me "Mom." He'd lost his mother to drugs when he was fourteen years old. His father was abusive and a career criminal.

I treated Anthony the same way I treated Keven. There was a solid bond between us, and even when he broke my trust, I could show him what forgiveness felt like. One time he woke up from a 48-hour coma on life support and found me sitting next to his hospital bed. When he realized I'd been there the whole time, he cried, "You really do love me!" Anthony's life was far different from Keven's. He was born into a family of substance users. His parents mostly used meth, but they also did other drugs. On his father's side, everyone had issues with drugs or alcohol.

Anthony and his immediate family also endured abuse from his father. I heard stories of Anthony trying to protect his mom and brother (Tim, two years younger) from his dad. As early as four years old, Ant learned the signs of impending abuse and would grab Tim and carry him up a tree to hide. It's hard to imagine living in fear of your own father.

At 5'9", he wasn't tall. Built like a boxer, he was solid and muscular with broad shoulders. Anthony had hazel eyes and a beautiful smile. He usually kept his hair very short or shaved his head. His hair was a kinky curly mop if he grew it out.

He had a way of drawing people to him. When he was present, there was always more laughter and never a dull moment. He played guitar and sang, wrote rap songs, was an excellent artist, and used his talent doing tattoos. He made friends wherever he went, and girls found him irresistible.

After a few years, Anthony and Keven realized they couldn't hang out with each other without getting into trouble or endangering themselves. They only saw each other when I was with them. If one was trying to get sober, he knew he had to stay away from the other. Often one was "locked up" or in rehab, and the other was with me.

Anthony didn't have a car, so I took him to appointments and gave him rides to various places. Riding around singing in the car (something Keven was not into) was so much fun. We'd run errands and go shopping. He loved home-cooked food, so he was often at our house for mealtime. Anthony was one of my mom's favorite people to cook for because of all the compliments he gave her.

Mostly, Anthony and I had deep conversations and encouraged each other through our struggles. There were many times I sat near hospital beds after ODs or injuries. (Between Keven and Anthony, I have been to almost every hospital in our county!)

During his time in jail and prison, I visited him and picked him up when he was released. I have an enormous stack of letters he sent me and some beautiful drawings he did while doing his time.

One night, Anthony called me, crying, saying he felt all alone in the world. I was in bed but got up, pulled on a jacket and jeans, and drove to the address he had given me. I stopped to buy him a pack of Camel Crush cigarettes, his favorite brand, something small to cheer him up. We stood under the black sky near the apartment where Anthony was crashing.

"I don't think I can last here much longer; life hurts too much," he said.

My arm was around him as he spoke those words, and we gazed upward. Then, a shooting star flashed across the sky. I'd never seen one that lasted so long and seemed so close.

"It's my mom!" he shouted ecstatically. "It's my mom! It's her right there!"

I knew a sign from his mom was a shooting star. He cried with joy and hope.

At 5 p.m. on September 7, 2015, my phone rang. It was Anthony's grandmother, whom I had grown very close to. "Can you come over now?" Dread swept over me when she said it. I didn't ask questions. "Please don't be dead," I chanted over and over on the short drive to his grandparent's house. Upon arriving, one look into their eyes told me he was gone.

A girl, Sarah, had left him unconscious in their rental car. They were in Las Vegas on their way to Colorado for his court date. There was an argument between them about him taking her anxiety medication. She refused to let him into their hotel room. At 11:20 a.m. the following day, they found him dead in the passenger seat. They ruled the death suspicious after a witness confirmed that Sarah called him, saying she thought Anthony was dying as she drove around and didn't know what to do. Later, when I went to visit the site where his life ended, the first thing I noticed was a hospital directly across the street from the hotel. I still haven't completely let go of my anger toward Sarah.

Losing Anthony gutted me. His death affected me more than any preceding loss. I was heartbroken. Also, I knew it would be a hundred times worse if I ever lost Keven. Ant's death led me to Solace for Hope. The group founded by Maggie Fleitman (I dedicated *Keven's Choice* to her.)

Keven's death changed everything in me—every cell in my body, every thought, every heartbeat. I would have felt so alone after losing both boys without Solace for Hope. When Keven passed, I'd been with the group for five years and considered them to be the only friends who understood what I'd been through. I knew my pain wasn't as deep as theirs because Anthony wasn't my birth son. They surrounded me with love and care after I lost Kev. In the back of this book, you will find the names of lost loved ones, many from Solace for Hope. Grief is something you don't have to do alone. If I could make only one suggestion to help a grieving person, it would be to find a support group, in person or online. Being understood is like a balm on the pain of loss.

BONUS CHAPTER 2

MY BOY KEVEN

I never planned on becoming a mother. I took a year off dating after breaking up with Jim, my boyfriend of three years. A little later that year, Jim asked me out for pizza and beer. One thing led to another, and the next thing I knew, a voice in my head told me, "You just got pregnant." No doubt in my mind, the voice (whoever it was) was right. Exactly nine months to the day later, Keven was born.

Jim offered to marry me and was relieved when I turned him down. We were no longer in love, and it would have been a mistake. Years later, I second-guessed this decision because Keven made it clear he felt he was missing out on many things by not having a dad. Jim did provide Kev with an older half-sister, Annie, who was sixteen when Keven was born, and a younger half-brother, Michael.

I started feeling single-parent guilt when Keven was two. At the park and on outings, I saw dads with their kids. Each time, my heart ached, especially if it was a father and son. As young as four, he started worrying about not having a man in his life to teach him "guy stuff," like using tools, shaving, and sports. My mom and sister helped me raise him. Even though he loved all three of us, he complained about living with only women.

Jim was not very involved in Keven's life, but fortunately, his parents treated Keven just like the rest of their grandchildren. They invited him to family celebrations and holidays, and he loved his aunts, uncles, cousins, and, of course, "Nana and Papa" and his half-siblings.

Over the years, I stayed close with Annie. She and Kev formed a deeper connection when he was in his twenties and Annie was in her forties. Sadly, drug use was something they had in common. Four months after Keven died, Annie passed away. Jim called to let me know, but I wasn't told and didn't ask about her exact cause of death. She'd had various health problems since childhood.

Michael looked up to Keven and thought he was "cool." Kev would often stop by his dad's house once he was old enough to drive, and he and Michael would hang out. On the last visit there, Michael admired a new ring Keven was wearing, a special gift from his Aunt Therese. Being Keven, he gave the ring to his brother; ever since he was a child, he often gave away his belongings. A few weeks later, after Keven's death, I realized the night he gave Michael the ring was the last time he saw him. I couldn't help but wonder if Keven knew he wouldn't be around much longer.

When he was in third grade, his teacher confirmed my worries about Keven's mood changes. She told me he hadn't been himself in class. The cheerful smile, the humor, and the enthusiasm for learning were gone. As someone with depression at the same age, I wanted to help him. The child psychiatrist suggested medication, but I wasn't comfortable with it, so I tried it myself. The anti-depressant allowed me to experience life without depression after battling the dark cloud that hovered over me my entire life. This helped me decide to try antidepressants for Keven. They helped him; he took them until 6th grade. Unfortunately, one of the side effects was weight gain which resulted in bullying from his classmates and caused more harm than the actual depression.

The bullying continued throughout the rest of elementary school. In sixth grade, he had a teacher who was the worst bully of them all. One day, she made an inappropriate comment to me, “I bet you sometimes wish you hadn't had him.” I was so shocked that I just walked away from her and then spent the rest of the year trying to remove him from her class. I went as far as the superintendent's office, and they still refused to move him. This was the first time I saw Keven get angry, and I wasn't used to it. He rarely expressed anger before Ms. Mean Teacher.

The summer between sixth and seventh grade, he grew almost six inches and lost all the weight. That year, he made new friends and caught the girls’ attention. Keven grew to be 6’1”, and with his green/blue eyes (they changed color) and dark hair, he was a good-looking young man. It was a great few years with only the everyday trials of life.

At age fifteen, some older guys on his high school wrestling team introduced Keven to drugs. It started with the usual marijuana and alcohol. I learned about it when he had his first run-in with law enforcement. A group of kids were partying at a park by our house, and a neighbor called it in. When the kids realized the cops were there, most of them ran and got away. They caught Keven and three other boys. It shocked me to see him in handcuffs when I arrived. The other boys sat quietly on the curb, waiting for their parents. Not my boy, he mouthed off to the police officers, which got him in more trouble. Alcohol caused Kev to be belligerent and out of control. Fortunately, he didn’t enjoy drinking and rarely drank after this incident.

The call that evening was the first of many. “Ma’am, we have your son detained.” When he was over eighteen, the calls changed to “Mom, I got busted. I’m in jail.” Those calls eventually became, “This is Global Tel Link. You are receiving a prepaid call from (Keven), an inmate at (jail or prison name). If you would like to accept this call, please say, or dial five now.” It became so frequent I set up an account so I’d always be able to take his and Anthony’s calls.

At seventeen, he met Jon, Kelly, and Anthony, his new friends. Jon and Anthony were older than Keven and attended community college. Anthony had a reputation that preceded him. I’d heard through some of Keven’s friends, “You never want to get in a fight with Anthony; he’s brutal.” However, all three of them were polite and friendly; it never crossed my mind that they were all using heroin.

One day when they were together, Kelly offered Keven heroin. Jon and Anthony warned him not to try it. They were both addicted and didn’t want to see him in the same dark place they were. But Kev gave in to the pretty girl with the syringe. Typically, a first-time user chooses to smoke or snort heroin, but Keven never did anything halfway and injected it his first time. This was an indicator of how serious his addiction would become, an early sign he would fight it for the rest of his life. The first time Keven was arrested, I was at his court proceedings. The judge called me to her bench to tell me she was keeping Keven in jail till a rehab bed opened for him. She said it was uncommon for a person his age to be such a hardcore user. She feared that if she let him out, he would have a serious risk of overdosing and dying.

In my book, *Keven’s Choice,* I detail what the next thirteen years were like for us. I talk about how it affected the entire family and how Keven’s anxiety and depression grew. The book doesn’t have a “happy ending,” but I wrote it to educate. I want families to see not only what a mentally ill substance user went through but the family's torment. I also shared my thoughts on topics like tough love, medically assisted treatment, and the detriments of prison. Looking back, I often wonder how I survived those years. The answer is the same as how I'm making it through his loss—you have no other choice. "One day at a time" is ingrained in my mind, as well as "One moment at a time."

Keven started hearing voices in his head in his early twenties. The voices told him he was a loser and sometimes told him to hurt himself. He believed a demon inhabited his bedroom and most nights slept elsewhere in the house. His drug use spiraled out of control to where he was living to get his next fix. Withdrawal from heroin or prescription opiates is excruciating. I saw firsthand how much pain he'd be in and how sick he'd be when he went through it at home. I usually paid for him to undergo a medical detox, easing his symptoms.

I lost track of all his time in jail and prison and how many rehabs, detoxes, and sober living homes he went to. There were many psychiatrists as well—because of the drug use, getting an accurate diagnosis was difficult, but they tried many medications. Keven also began having a deep sense of self-loathing. His last psychiatrist noted this, along with his suicidal ideation. He'd made several attempts over the years and warned me it would end this way. With each attempt, he spent time in the mental hospital and came out with a handful of prescriptions. Unfortunately, the meds didn't help for two reasons: first, he'd keep using drugs while taking the prescriptions, and second, the side effects (impaired cognitive function, drowsiness, and weight gain) were hard to live with.

We tried every avenue of treatment for both the addiction and mental illness. Nothing helped him. This is where some might think to themselves, "Yes, you tried everything, but did he want help? Did he try hard enough? Recovery is available to those who want it. He must not have wanted it enough." I can see where this assumption comes from.

Sometimes, a person dies from an overdose before they find sobriety. In cases of mental illness combined with addiction, there is an added element of danger. Keven's hopelessness outweighed his desire to "get clean" and have a future. It tormented him to see how much turmoil he created for his family and how messed up his life was. Along with addiction usually comes stealing, lying, and committing various crimes to support drug use. He had a felony record and new charges for a DUI (he was at a gas station doing drugs in his car, blacked out, and the car rolled into the building. There was no damage done, but someone called the police, and they arrested him.) It became his way of life; he fought it as hard as he could. At other times, he felt he was a hopeless cause and wouldn't bother trying.

My life changed forever the moment I heard the gunshot coming from his bedroom on the morning of August 11, 2020. I went from a broken-hearted mom filled with worry to a mom who didn't want to go on without the love of her life. Time doesn't heal all wounds but creates distance from the torment of early grief. It never gets easier, but it becomes more manageable.

To my boy: Keven, I am grateful to be your mom. I love you.

RESOURCES

GRIEF GROUPS

Loss of a Child: The Compassionate Friends - Support after the death of a child (online)
www.grief.com
www.griefshare.org
www.griefincommon.com
www.solaceforhope.org (local and online)

SUICIDE AWARENESS/PREVENTION

Dial 988 for Suicide Hotline
The American Foundation for Suicide Prevention:
www.afsp.org
The Trevor Project: www.thetrevorproject.org
Alliance of Hope: https://allianceofhope.org

MENTAL HEALTH

Dial 988 for Mental Health Crisis
NAMI - National Alliance for Mental Illness
National Institute for Mental Health
SAMSHSA -Substance Abuse Mental Health Services Administration

SUBSTANCE USE DISORDER

Alcoholics Anonymous
Smart Recovery
Shatterproof
Partnership To End Addiction
SAMSHSA -Substance Abuse Mental Health Services Administration
Substance Use Resources for Adolescents and Young Adults

SUPPORT FOR CAREGIVERS

Home | The National Alliance for Caregiving
Find Local Caregiver Resources and Support In Your State (aarp.org)

TRAUMA INTERVENTION PROGRAMS (TIP)

"TIP is a team of specially trained volunteers called to scenes by emergency personnel to provide emotional support and practical resources to anyone experiencing a traumatic incident. Available 24 hours a day, 365 days a year, TIP has become an integral part of the emergency response system in over 250 cities nationwide. This is since its inception in 1985 in San Diego County.

TIP provides assistance to family members, friends, witnesses, bystanders, crime victims, and anyone impacted by a traumatic event. These include sudden or unexpected deaths, traffic accidents, drownings, suicides, overdoses, sexual assault, fire, home invasions, and mass casualty events.

TIP has received the prestigious Innovation Award in State and Local Government from Harvard University and the Ford Foundation. It also received the Crime Victim Service Award from the US Justice Department and the Governor's Victim Service Award from the State of California."

NOTE FROM THE AUTHOR

Being a TIP volunteer has been a big part of my life since I joined them. I can't speak highly enough of this wonderful organization. If you're interested in learning more about the organization and/or volunteer opportunities, visit their website:

Trauma Intervention Programs - Home (tipnational.org)

FURTHER READING

It's OK That You're Not OK: Meeting Grief and Loss in a Culture That Doesn't Understand
Megan Devine (October 2007, Sounds True, Inc.)

Finding Meaning: The Sixth Stage of Grief
David Kessler (November 2019, Scribner)

Healing After Loss: Daily Meditations For Working Through Grief

Martha Whitmore Hickman (December 1994, William Morrow)

Deactivate Your Survival Trances: Three Ways to Restore Your Life after Trauma
Shuna Morelli (August 16, 2022, BodyMind Bridge Institute)

ACKNOWLEDGMENTS

The process of writing a book can be lonely. It's definitely a roller-coaster ride filled with doubt, joy, frustration and hopefully satisfaction. These are the people who kept me going and helped shape this book with their stories and encouragement. I am grateful to each of you!

- Therese Legere, my favorite sister and number one encourager!
- Kathy Scruton, you picked me up whenever I fell into doubt!
- Peter Heymans—Peter, your friendship is full of love and support; you got me through another book!
- Maggie Fleitman and Solace for Hope—you are my family. No one can understand unless they've been in our shoes.
- Phil Stockwell—Phil, you are my living memory of both Anthony and Keven. Hugging you is the next best thing to hugging them.
- Timothy Gager and the Inner Circle writing group, past and present, my tribe! You give me the courage and drive to keep going!
- Jill Carlyle—Jill, I couldn't ask for more in an editor/publisher. You went above and beyond and were accessible to me every single step of the way.

This book would not be what it is without your professionalism and talent. I am most grateful for your dedication and passion; having someone care as much about the book as I do is incredible; this is *our* book. I will treasure this experience and our friendship forever.

- Keven and Anthony–I miss you guys so damn much! I can't see you, but I feel you near me. You will always be at the center of my life.

A very special thanks for their contributions:

Bob Edwards
Donna Van Horn
Ellie Markes
Harv Jamison
Heidi Le
Laura Swank
Lee Varon
Margie Allman
Mike Duffy
Paul Lesinski
Stephanie Swanson

Readers—Thank you sincerely for reading this book! I invite you to send me your stories about loved ones you've lost and/or words that have comforted you or upset you. I have a blog and would love to include your experiences. If you enjoyed it or not, I would appreciate a review on Amazon, Barnes & Noble, or Goodreads.

I can be reached at barbaralegere@gmail.com, and look forward to hearing from you!

About the Author

Photo: Kenny Goldberg

Barbara Legere is the bestselling author of *Keven's Choice* and co-author of the bestselling anthology *The Epiphanies Project*. Her writing has been featured in *Prevention Magazine, Salon, Huffington Post*, and *Authority Magazine* for her work in advocating for those suffering from substance abuse, mental health issues, and grief. In addition, she is a sought-after podcast guest speaking on grief awareness, suicide prevention, and compassion for substance abuse disorder. She is a volunteer for the national non-profit TIP (Traumatic Intervention Program). Legere lives in Southern California with her sister, cat, tortoise, and three dogs. More of her writing and podcast interviews can be found on barbaralegere.com. *Talk To Me I'm Grieving* is her second book.